Pike and Freshwater Predator Fishing in the British Isles

Pike and Freshwater Predator Fishing in the British Isles

Edit... gowski

Quiller

Copyright © 2008 Dr Steve Rogowski

First published in the UK in 2008
by Quiller, an imprint of Quiller Publishing Ltd

British Library Cataloguing-in-Publication Data
A catalogue record for this book
is available from the British Library

ISBN 978 1 84689 043 7

Printed in China

Quiller
An imprint of Quiller Publishing Ltd
Wykey House, Wykey, Shrewsbury, SY4 1JA
Tel: 01939 261616 Fax: 01939 261606
E-mail: info@quillerbooks.com
Website: www.countrybooksdirect.com

Contents

Foreword

One might ask: 'Why another book on fishing for freshwater predators, especially pike?' The truth is that the sport changes so quickly these days; you only have to subscribe to *Pike and Predators* magazine for a year and you will see what I mean. We do need a staging post now and again, a place where what is known and unknown can be gathered together and presented to anglers for examination. This book is like that. It brings together some of the leading experts in the fields of fishing for pike, catfish, eels, perch and zander, and they tell us where we are at, and what the problems and questions of the future might be. The contributions are written in such a way, and edited by Steve Rogowski in such a manner, that the foregoing is certainly fully achieved. The reader will find invaluable information and advice about these species themselves, together with actually fishing for them. Tackle, methods, techniques, fishing stories and more are all covered. Furthermore, the book manages to knit together the whole field of predator fishing in freshwater, including chub, trout and salmon, in the overall context of the sport. In so doing it does a great service to the angler.

Some might say it is not exactly a book for beginners, perhaps demanding of the reader a certain level of initial knowledge, but Steve is at pains to get the fundamentals correct so that an angler of any experience or persuasion will be helped. The book also touches on many matters which could be considered by some as peripheral to the sport of freshwater predator fishing, but nonetheless these issues are well worth airing. For example, it touches on eating the catch. I completely agree with Steve that anglers should retain the right to cook and eat their catch. What is the point of being a human being, a hunter, if you cannot eat, if you sometimes choose, the results of your efforts. Mind you, I have always thought that the advice regarding cooking pike is that they should be small (and 'sweet'!) is complete nonsense. The best pike weight for cooking is around 12 to 15 lb, which I imagine might make a few people blanch.

There is also a nice discussion, indeed essay, on global warming and the effects it might have on fishing in the British Isles. I enjoyed that. As it happens I do not fully agree with Steve, because it seems to me that the current phase of global warming began about twenty thousand years ago and it is going to continue a while yet! It is perhaps debateable (or it would not be being debated) whether the recent addition of humans to the equation has had much effect, and if it has whether anything much can be done about it. Nevertheless this section forms part of a terrific chapter, one which any sentient angler will surely enjoy.

The section on anti-anglers is well argued but, perhaps, Steve is a little too kind to them. I do not think for a moment that the anti-anglers (at least, not those who disrupt fishing) acknowledge that anglers are conservationists, or that we have tended the rivers unaided for centuries. They are anarchists, pure and simple are they not? And at the moment, of course, many have found another bandwagon to ride on, namely that flying the banner of global warming! This is what makes this book such an enjoyable and fascinating read. It deals with predator fishing in fresh water in the British Isles but it does so in a full social context.

Somebody once told me, when I was very young, that *all* fish species are predatory. And that is true: I have caught tench which disgorged small tench and roach which disgorged baby roach. I recently caught, fairly and squarely I might add, a 6 lb tench on a large plug and I have had double-figure commons on spinners. But the editor and contributors of this book are right to confine themselves to the major predators, whilst at the same time acknowledging that the time might well come…

Barrie Rickards
Cambridge, November 2007

Acknowledgements

As usual, initially it is the contributors that I wish to thank for their help and support throughout this project, along with Barrie Rickards who agreed to write the Foreword and also made some helpful comments.

Others who deserve a mention for their help, whether they realise it or not, are Adam, Michael and Tim Rogowski, Danny Haynes, 'Spinning' Steve Appleby, Shaun Cunnane, Brian Steele, Steve Whybrow, Mark Goddard, Richard Young, Peter Hague, Dick Culpin and Bill Palmer. Lastly, but certainly not least, there are Lynda Bardsley and Pat Dixon. I know it is the twenty-first century but, putting it mildly, I remain a bit of a techno-phobe, and these two women certainly helped me with my computer and in other ways as well.

Photographs are copyright of the editor and contributors.

As is always the case, I bear full responsibility for any mistakes or inaccuracies that the reader may find.

Steve Rogowski
Oldham, December 2007

1
Introduction:

Pike and Freshwater Predator Fishing in the British Isles
Steve Rogowski

Pike and freshwater predator fishing is one of the most popular and exciting forms of angling not only in the British Isles but also in much of Europe and North America. As I write this I have just come back from Canada (not a fishing trip I might add but to see the Rolling Stones) where I met an enthusiastic angler who was at pains to tell me about his experiences of catching 'northern pike', the equivalent of our pike. The muskellunge, another relative of our pike, and walleye, a relative of our zander, are also very popular fish in parts of Canada and the USA. Then again as far as Europe is concerned, pike are widely distributed and fine examples of the fishing potential are Sweden and Germany. Paradoxically, bearing in mind we are discussing freshwater predators, Sweden is a destination for many after Baltic Sea pike. Catfish, eels, perch and zander are also common in much of Europe and fished for as a result. But as the title indicates it is the British Isles that are the focus of this book, and the popularity of pike and freshwater predator fishing is evidenced by the thriving membership of clubs that cover pike as well as the other predator fish referred to. They have members who are dedicated, even obsessed, by catching these particular species of fish. What is more, anglers who target one particular species are also likely to target one or more of the others. Mark Barrett, for example, loves his perch fishing but also targets pike and zander, while Neville Fickling is primarily known as a pike angler but he is equally at home catching zander. Likewise Steve Ormrod's favourite species is pike but he also loves to catch eels and more recently catfish. And while I also spend a lot of time trying to catch pike, sometimes with success I might add, catching a large eel, perch or zander is equally thrilling and enjoyable.

What then attracts so many anglers to pike and freshwater predator fishing? And before trying to answer that question one must remember why so many go fishing in the first place. Another key question is why the species referred to are primarily considered as predator fish worthy of fishing for. One has only to recall that other fresh-water fish sometime predate but are not generally targeted as such, and others still, though generally not regarded as predator fish can, in certain circumstances, be caught as such. Others relate to why pike, catfish, eels, perch and zander are deemed to warrant separate chapters in a book such as this, as opposed to others like chub, trout and salmon. There are no easy answers to all this as the reader will see, but having addressed such questions in this chapter I briefly look at pike, catfish, eels, perch and zander as well as giving equally brief comments on fishing for them. I emphasise brief because these species are dealt with more fully in their respective chapters. Thereafter there are longer sections on the aforementioned chub, trout and salmon including fishing for them using predator methods. Finally, I end this chapter with a discussion of the organisation of the book itself; individual chapters follow on the main freshwater predator species referred to and a concluding chapter which outlines some of the challenges for pike and freshwater predator fishing in the British Isles at the beginning of the new millennium. Despite these challenges, I then look at future prospects and overall end on an optimistic note.

The Attractions of Pike and Freshwater Predator Fishing

A first question to consider then, is why do people actually go fishing and freshwater predator fishing in particular? As Jens Ploug Hansen and Goran Cederberg point out in *The Complete Book of Spinning and Baitcasting* people have fished, hunted and gathered for many, many thousands of years, even though it is only relatively recently that we have had the privilege to fish for pleasure. For example, barbed hooks made of bone and wood were made as early as 30,000 BC and by 2000 BC the Egyptians were using hooks and basic rods. Theocritus provided some evidence suggesting that the Greeks fished for pleasure round about 300 BC, while the Chinese were fishing with rods and silk lines around AD 200.

In the fifteenth century Juliana Berners' *Treatyse of Fysshynge with an Angle* was written and provided practical details about fishing as a sport as well as philosophical details about the fisherman's attitude towards nature. Then Izaak Walton's classic *The Compleat Angler* appeared in 1653, this firmly establishing fishing as a recreation and means of pleasure and enjoyment, also pointing out that the experience of nature was as important as the catch. Importantly though it must be remembered that much of this only applied to the upper classes as the majority of people, being poor and often exploited, were forced to make better use of fishing and fish.

But nowadays fishing is certainly about far more than simply catching fish. It is about getting away from the daily grind and leaving the stress of everyday work and life behind. Although it can be a struggle in the depths of winter, most would agree about the delights of awaking before dawn and setting off so you near the water as day breaks. And once the tackling up has been done and the rods cast out, appreciation of one's location together with the sights and sounds of nature really does sink in. Dependent on the time of day and seasons of the year these can range from the sight of a ghostly, swooping barn owl over a Yorkshire river or a golden eagle soaring over the Highlands of Scotland, to magnificent pine and deciduous forests or heather-strewn moorland hills. Or again there are the beautiful mountains and hills surrounding the western

This is what pike and freshwater predator fishing is all about – Steve Rogowski with a pristine, beautifully marked pike.

But companionships also come into play: three-quarters of the Rogowski clan, Michael, Tim and Steve, with Adam not managing to make this trip.

loughs of Ireland or lakes of Wales, which can be contrasted with the peaceful vista of land and water, together with flights of wildfowl, which form the Norfolk Broads. Although many anglers, including myself, are happy to enjoy all of this on their own, such experiences are a great way to build, rekindle or cement friendships and companionships. One has only to recall the obvious example that father-son, brother-brother, uncle-nephew relationships are often formed and bolstered through all of this. Fortunately and increasingly so these days women are also often included.

But, as I said, it is not just about catching fish, much as we all want to do this. It is also about having a laugh and joke along the way, as well as more thoughtful, even philosophical discussions. However, apart from the picturesque backdrop and social side to fishing, there is another essential ingredient to the enjoyment, namely the challenge. You may be pitting your wits in a variety of ways including against a difficult venue, inclement weather, your companion and, not least, your target species. Cracking a hard water by catching your target in such as rain and gale lashed conditions, and perhaps beating your companion in the process, certainly does provide a great sense of satisfaction and enjoyment.

Having looked at some of the attractions of fishing generally, what is it that attracts anglers to fishing for pike and freshwater predator fish in particular? Perhaps it is because when any youngster starts out fishing the first and easiest fish they are likely to catch will be a tiny but voracious perch. My earliest fishing forays in Yorkshire, such as on the River Ure at Ripon, Castle Howard Lake near York, and Clayton Ponds on

A voracious perch which took this spoon.

The fearsome head and jaws of a pike.

the outskirts of Leeds, all involved the capture of many of these attractive, greedy fish. But perhaps there is a more profound reason that attracts us to freshwater predator fishing. As indicated above, mankind started as hunters and gatherers, and similarly by their very nature predator fish are hunters so maybe there is something primordial in our fascination for this aspect of angling. Surely it is not too far fetched to say that we actually had/do have something in common with these predators: many, many generations ago our ancestors hunted for food and were thus living their lives in a similar fashion to these primeval fish.

Then there is the physical appearance and aggressive nature of these freshwater predator fish to consider. Who cannot be captivated by the streamlined body and fearsome jaws and teeth of the pike, or be enthralled by the handsome stripes and spiny dorsal fin of the perch? Even the snake-like eel, and almost equally snake-like catfish, both of which I have heard called 'the devil's own work', have something fascinating about them. This last comment even applies despite the fact that one book I read referred to 'the hideous Wels' when discussing the catfish. In addition though, the zander and its two dorsal fins, one spiny, together with large jaws, teeth and eyes is almost as fearsome as the pike. Overall perhaps it is these predators' way of life, appearance and, not least, ability to grow large and fight hard that attracts so many of us into wanting to fish for them.

13

Steve Rogowski admires a nice double figure pike.

A 30 or 40 lb pike may well be beyond the reach of most of us, but a double figure or even a 20 lb pike is not and will certainly give you a good scrap. Eels, perch and zander do not grow as large, of course, but hooking anything over 2 lb in the case of eels and perch, and, say, 6 lb in the case of zander together with the right tackle will certainly let you know you have caught a decent fish. Then we have catfish which are the largest of all these freshwater predator fish in the British Isles growing to over 100 lb, though perhaps a more realistic target is 20 lb; a fish like this will certainly test your gear. Such factors do certainly help explain why I go fishing for such predators, in addition to the attractions of angling more generally.

One might, for instance, arrive with a friend on a remote Scottish loch at dawn on a cold but bright autumnal day hoping to catch that elusive monster pike. Both of us are filled with a great sense of anticipation as to what the day might bring. The loch is flat calm and the sun is beginning to rise over the hills and pine forest of the far bank. The rods are quickly set up and the baits cast out; the laughs and jokes start as the waiting begins. Two inquisitive swans arrive during the morning looking for thrown away scraps of food, and seagulls occasionally visit looking for the same. But as far as the fishing is concerned, several contemplative and relaxing hours later the bite alarms have not made a single bleep and the drop-back indicators have remained unmoved. Nevertheless we fish on in the hope that eventually a big pike will find and wolf down one of the baits. Then, out of the blue and while thoughts are turning to the long journey home, what better sight and sound is there than when the drop-back trembles before the line is stripped away and the bite-alarm screams continuously. It does not really matter if it is your rod or your friend's. The long wait is over as the rod is grabbed and the reel cranked, tightening the line in the process, before striking into an unyielding fish. She runs powerfully to the left and right before gradually coming to the net. Finally a tail-walk and shake of the formidable head and jaws takes place before the capture is complete and another fine specimen is landed. Not a thirty, of course, but still a fine double figure pike. Congratulations take place and it goes without saying that she has been well worth the wait.

Or again, one might arrive alone at the river on a humid summer's evening in the hope of catching some large eels. It is quiet and peaceful apart from the occasional sound of a couple of oystercatchers, and confidence is high. After catching some small roach and gudgeon these are knocked on the head ready to be used as bait as soon as dusk approaches. An hour or so later, as the sun slowly sets, two rods are cast out both with the fresh deadbaits on; one goes into a deep pool at the margin near an

Steve Rogowski's rods are set on Loch Garry.

This 2 lb plus River Ure eel fell to Steve Rogowski on ledgered worms.

overhanging tree, the other is cast to bushes on the far bank. It begins to get dark but it is still warm as the bats make their silent appearance and an owl hoots in the distance. Suddenly the bite alarm on the margin rod beeps and is away as the deadbait is snaffled. The rod is grasped, the fish struck into and several shuddery runs later a fine 2 lb plus eel is landed. A can of beer is quickly opened in silent celebration and the rod recast; the action has begun. Three more are landed during the night, the largest being a little short of 3 lb, before dawn slowly approaches. It is soon time to pack up quietly before making the journey home. It has certainly been a successful and enjoyable night not least because the rain and thunder storms kept away.

Why Pike, Catfish, Eels, Perch and Zander?

The dictionary definition of 'predator' is an animal, or in our case a fish, that preys naturally on others. As such there are many freshwater fish that could come under this category as Cynthia Davies and colleagues note in their book *Freshwater Fishes in Britain*. For example, the three-spined stickleback will eat the fry of other fish, and the river lamprey of Loch Lomond are known to feed on powan. Similarly barbel will eat small fish, notably gudgeon, while carp and bream are known to pick up deadbaits; in fact not long ago I caught an 11 lb mirror carp that took a liking for a lamprey section meant for pike. Arctic charr also eat small fish and can be caught using small spinners as well as by fly-fishing. However, all of these species usually feed on such as aquatic insect larvae, algae, zoo plankton and plant material. Consequently they are not generally the target of predator anglers, and in any case the reader will wholeheartedly agree that predator fishing for a stickleback is hardly practical or worth the effort! No, the targets for freshwater predator anglers in the British Isles are the five species I keep coming back to, namely pike, catfish, eels, perch and zander. All of these prey on other fish wholly or as part of their normal diet. In fact, pike and zander feed on little else other than fish, hence their technical name is piscavores. Catfish, eels and perch eat other fish much of the time and can be said to be predatory in nature or having predatory tendencies at times. Hopefully then, it is not hard to see why these species feature heavily in this book.

An 11 lb mirror carp that took a liking to Steve Rogowski's lamprey section meant for pike.

17

A nice perch which took Steve Rogowski's ledgered bleak on the River Ure.

Others that sometimes prey on other fish are chub, trout and salmon. Chub normally feed on insect larvae and crustaceans but the larger fish also consume small fish such as minnows and gudgeon. Trout, and here I include both brown and sea trout, generally feed on aquatic and terrestrial invertebrates but they will also take small fish like minnows. Importantly though the 'ferox' brown trout of large, deep lakes, lochs and loughs have a diet which consists entirely of other fish. Finally, salmon also feed on aquatic and terrestrial invertebrates as juveniles but on migrating to the sea they eat fish before returning to freshwater rivers to spawn, this being when they can be caught using predator fishing methods.

One might ask that if chub, trout and salmon sometimes eat fish and can be caught using predator fishing methods why is there not a separate chapter for each of them in this book? The simple answer is that they are more usually fished for using coarse fishing methods in the case of chub, and game fishing methods, not least fly-fishing, in the case of trout and salmon. In addition, generally they do not have the fearsome or aggressive reputation of the above five predators. Arguably then they do not merit a chapter of their own in a book such as this. However, as they are still fished for using predator fishing methods, I deal with this here in this introductory chapter. Some readers may disagree with this stance but I trust they will at least understand and appreciate my reasoning. First though, let me have a brief look at the five main freshwater predators of the British Isles referred to together with equally brief comments on fishing for them.

Pike

Beginning with the pike, or *Esox lucius* to use the scientific name, it is the largest natural freshwater predator in the British Isles and a more popular quarry than ever before. They live and thrive in many different waters, both still and flowing, thus being very widely distributed; indeed, I have caught them in England, Scotland, Wales and Ireland. Spawning occurs in shallow water and the fry live on invertebrates before moving to fish. They grow quickly as they spend their lives mostly where the prey fish are, but not surprisingly the availability and size of prey fish influences growth rates. Having a vigorous appetite they are a very efficient prey-eating machine, for instance often lying waiting for an unsuspecting roach or perch to pass before it is quickly engulfed. One only has to recall the streamlined body with all the power in the tail,

Dick Culpin with a personal best 28 lb pike from the Lake of Menteith.

A magnificent 42 lb catfish caught in France by Danny Haynes, but you can catch them like this in Britain too.

the camouflage markings and the large head, jaws and teeth. All this, together with their size and hard-fighting qualities explain why so many want to fish for them. And mentioning fishing for them, this involves baitfishing, both dead and livebaits, together with lure fishing including fly-fishing. Although I have lure fished and had some success into the bargain, if truth is told I am really a committed dead and live-baiter as such utilising float, ledgering and paternostering methods. As with all pike fishing, these require strong, specialist tackle which can cope with the surging runs and tail-walking of a large pike.

Catfish

Catfish, *Silurus glanis*, are more correctly called the Wels, Danube or European catfish. They are native to continental Europe, notably the Danube Basin but were brought to England in the 1860s. They are now in lakes and other stillwaters throughout England together with a few in Wales, also having spread to some rivers probably by flooding. It is the elongated body with smooth, scale-less skin coated in mucus that everyone associates with catfish. They also have a broad, flat head with nostrils set far apart and small eyes, but a large mouth with barbels on the upper and lower jaws. Spawning occurs when the water reaches 19°C with invertebrates forming the diet of the juveniles before giving way to other fish, molluscs and crayfish. They mainly scavenge on the bottom but also rise to the surface for such as amphibians, and small mammals as well as fish. Maturing after about five years they are tough and persistent fighters when caught, this being done using, for example, dead and livebaits though lures are also successful despite the fish's relatively poor eyesight and its liking for murky water. Again the need for strong, specialist tackle needs to be emphasised.

Eels

The eel, to be precise the European eel, *Anguilla anguilla*, might well be the bane of match and pleasure anglers because of the tangled mess it makes of their tackle. But the bigger fish do put up a dogged, incessant fight, so it is no wonder many predator anglers target them. They have slimy, snakelike bodies with anal and dorsal fins merged together. Their mysterious and complicated life begins and ends in the Sargasso Sea south-west of Bermuda in the Atlantic Ocean. They are unpigmented (glass eels) as

This 1 lb plus eel was caught on ledgered worms from the River Ouse soon after dawn by Steve Rogowski.

juveniles in the spring as they arrive, but as they begin to swim up our rivers they change with the dorsal area becoming dark, brownish-green with the ventral surface becoming lighter, sometimes yellow (yellow eels). Mature eels, as they migrate seawards then become dark on the back and silvery or white underneath (silver eels). In freshwater they are ubiquitous being found in virtually all still and flowing water though the bigger fish prefer lowland lakes and rivers where there is plenty of cover and the bottom is muddy. Spending many years in freshwater before they return to the sea, they live on such as snails, insect larvae and fish. Although they can be caught by usual coarse fishing methods like float and ledgered maggots, for the larger fish small live or dead fish and worms are a better bet. My bigger eels have come mainly from Yorkshire rivers such as the Ouse or Ure, but also the Norfolk Broads and the Lake District. Dead ledgered small roach have been successful, but also paternostered live gudgeon and even ledgered mackerel tails meant for pike. Tackle needs to be strong enough to cope with the dogged surges of a large eel though it does not have to be on the scale needed for such as pike and catfish.

Perch

Perch, *Perca fluviatilis*, is an attractive, colourful fish hence one of its nicknames being the 'dandy'. There is the deep body, with usually four to six vertical bars or stripes over olive green flanks, together with a cream, sometimes orange, belly. Then there are the two dorsal fins the most prominent being opaque and armed with sharp spines. Finally, there is the large, armoured head with a big mouth containing numerous small teeth. They spawn in early spring when the water reaches 10°C. From an early age they readily eat fry before moving to larger fish, including each other, but they also eat aquatic invertebrates and terrestrial insects. Being very common they are found in most rivers and stillwaters throughout the British Isles and at a variety of depths from the shallows to the deeps. They are gregarious, shoaling fish, especially the smaller ones, though the larger specimens are more solitary often living in deep, dark haunts but within striking distance of prey. Fishing for such larger fish often involves worms and small coarse livebaits though coarse deads and lures, especially the latter work well. For example, I have had perch to over 3 lb on the Yorkshire Ouse using paternostered live gudgeon and skimmer bream. Other decent fish have fallen to paternostered live roach and perch on reservoirs in north-west England. My nephew Adam caught a magnificent 4 lb 8 oz specimen on a Toby lure while lure fishing for pike on the Ouse. It would have been the official record of the York Amalgamated Anglers section of the river, and perhaps the whole river for that matter, but I was the only witness and unfortunately another was also required.

Zander

I now come to the last of the freshwater predator fish that form the bulk of this book, namely the zander, *Sander lucioperca* or *Stizostedion lucioperca*, which is also known as the 'pikeperch'. It originated in central and eastern Europe from where it was introduced to two English lakes in 1878. In 1963 they were introduced to the Great Ouse Relief Channel, Norfolk from where they colonised the Fenland rivers. In 1976 it was evident they were in the Rivers Severn and Trent together with the canal system of the English midlands. Their spread continues to this day including to such as the River Thames and some lakes in the south-east of England. They are greenish-brown fish with darkish vertical bars on the flanks and they do resemble a cross between a pike and a perch. As such they also have two dorsal fins similar to the perch's as well as large jaws with fangs and teeth. They spawn between April and June, with the young fish feeding on fleas and plankton before moving mainly on to other fish. When it comes to fishing for them, tackle and methods are similar, though scaled down, to those used for pike, namely float, paternostered and ledgered coarse live and dead baits, though sea deads also work, as do lures. I have done my, albeit rather limited, zander fishing on the Fens particularly on the Great Ouse, Middle Level Drain and Roswell Pits. Even so it is worth noting that ledgered dead whole and half roach, and skimmer bream have proved particularly successful.

A ledgered half roach bait led to this 7 lb 8 oz zander for Steve Rogowski from the Fens' Middle Level Drain.

Having provided a brief overview of the main freshwater predators, it is timely to turn, in a little more detail, to the three other species that also predate at times and are thus fished for using predator fishing methods and tactics: the aforementioned chub, trout and salmon. At the outset, I want to emphasise that if using predator fishing methods for these species, and if pike are likely to be about, then a wire trace should be used. Importantly this will prevent bite-offs of tackle and resultant possible damage to the pike.

Chub

Keighley Angling Club Committee member Richard Young is passionate about chub and his chub fishing as the following shows:

My love for chub and chub fishing stems back to my early years when I first fished the winter on Yorkshire's River Aire. I vividly remember those initial sessions which were bitterly cold and demoralisingly fruitless. In fact, if my good friend and excellent angler David Windle had not assured me they were really there, I would have sworn I was fishing an empty river. Finally though, one Sunday morning I managed a super 4 lb plus fish on bread flake from the tail of a pool shrouded by snow-laden willows. That fish, laying cradled in my landing net on such a lead grey day could never know the elation I felt at its capture. All those hours I had spent looking transfixed at a motionless quiver tip over a river seemingly devoid of life, and then the long walks back home in the dark with painfully cold feet and freezing fingers sticking to the metal bankstick; all this disappeared in the euphoria of the moment of catching that first chub.

Many years have passed since then, and experience and learning have both helped all my angling to be much more consistent and successful. Today, fishing for new species or bigger specimen fish, together with fishing new venues, still hold all the mystery and excitement as they did when I was a youth. But overall I get the most pleasure from the anticipation of my winter chub fishing. Any success I have continues to feel a real accomplishment, this probably due to those early strivings on what is still considered to be a difficult river.

It goes without saying that chub are catchable throughout the season by just about every method and technique available to the angler. For instance, I have caught my favourite quarry on baits such as bread, maggots and casters through to designer baits like paste and pellets, all of which have either been float fished or ledgered. On long summer days when fish become fixed on emerging insects or floating terrestrials, I have caught using dry flies. Floating crust is another thrilling way to tempt them, as is using small livebaits, plugs and spinners. Takes can even be induced by twitching or pulling normal static, bottom-fished baits and this really can get you out of jail on a slow day. Despite all this, and the other baits and techniques available to the angler, even when you think you have worked it all out, chub can still prove to be the most infuriatingly difficult fish to catch.

Bronze and beautiful – a 5 lb 10 oz chub from the River Aire for Richard Young.

I think the reader will agree that Richard has neatly encapsulated why many are so fascinated with this particular species of fish.

The chub, *Leuciscus cephalus*, is also known locally by various other names such as loggerhead, chavender, chevin, alderman, and skelly. Growing to over the 9 lb mark in weight it is not surprising they are the target for many specimen anglers albeit, as Richard pointed out, such anglers usually tend to target them using coarse fishing methods and baits such as float or ledgered maggots, worms, slugs, luncheon meat, cheese and various paste and pellet-type products. But as we will see, more obvious predator methods and tactics come into play, these producing decent, hard-fighting fish.

Chub have a grey-green/grey-brown back with silvery flanks when young and are easily confused with dace, but they become yellower and then bronze in maturity. The belly is generally cream and the dorsal and tail fins range from grey to almost black, while those on the underside are yellow/orange/pink. The body is elongated and sturdy so it is not surprising they are a sporting fish. Both dorsal and anal fins are convex-edged and they have a large head with a large, thick-lipped mouth while the body scales are of a large metallic appearance.

Male chub mature at three to four years and the females a little later, with spawning usually taking place in shallow riffles over stones, gravel or weed to which the eggs stick. It occurs in May or June when large shoals congregate often with three or four males to each female. The eggs hatch in five to nine days depending on water temperature. After a year they can be 4 to 6 inches in length, attaining 8 to 10 inches within the next year and a couple of years later they can be 3 lb plus. As I said earlier, insect larvae, crustaceans and plant material are the initial foodstuffs but eventually large chub, the ones predator anglers want, consume small fish, frogs and crayfish. Incidentally, fruit and berries are also often eaten when they fall into the water.

As for their distribution, they are found in much of southern Britain but not in the far south-west of England, the westerly flowing rivers in Wales and most of Scotland. They are also absent from Ireland although they are said to have put in an appearance in such as the River Blackwater. It is the lowland and middle reaches of rivers, where the flow is moderate, that are the ideal habitats of chub. When young they congregate in large shoals and inhabit the surface layers though as they mature they become more solitary and predatory, preferring deeper pools where there is some cover. They are fond of gravel reaches and hard bottoms but also make the most of mud and harder clays. The older fish tend to reside in particular places, such as deeper pools with cover where they make foraging expeditions along the reach, returning regularly to their holes under the bank or beneath tree roots. They also like bridges though often preferring the faster water which brings down food. When the floods arrive they take to eddies and more sheltered places but remain nearer the stream rather than the slack itself.

Although traditionally associated with rivers, they are also found in stillwaters where they have been introduced or become isolated there by earthworks or river improvement schemes. They certainly achieve good growth rates here but whether they can breed successfully remains uncertain.

Having written that chub are largely absent from Scotland, it reminds me of a salmon fishing trip I once made to the River Annan in the south-west of the country. I was using a Toby lure and all of a sudden I hit what I thought was a snag. To my surprise though, the 'snag' slowly began to move upstream and sidewards in a strange sort of way. It did not feel like a fish let alone a salmon. Eventually my nephew Adam and I managed to get the culprit to the bank only to find that I had foul-hooked a 4 lb chub in its tail. Though not the salmon I wanted it was still very gratifying and at least I had caught what turned out to be my only fish of the day. In passing, the only other fish of the day also turned out not to be a salmon; my brother Mike caught his first pike for some thirty years, this being a small jack that took a liking for another Toby lure.

When it comes to fishing for chub, as stated, traditional coarse methods predominate, though pole fishing is also used notably on stillwaters. For example, traditional river fishing involves an 11 or 12 ft float or an 11 or 12 ft Avon quiver tip rod (in test curve terms about 1.25 lb will suffice), a matched small fixed spool reel holding 6 to 8 lb monofilament line, a float or ledger weights/swimfeeder with, say, a size 10 hook to 4 lb hook link. Many a chub can and are caught using such tackle and tactics, but it is more overt predator fishing methods that are our concern here. Although chub do occasionally pick up a deadbait meant for pike, the two main methods used for chub are livebaiting and lure fishing.

Livebaiting using a float can be an excellent method for tempting a large chevin. Light pike tackle can be used such as an 11 ft rod with a 2/2.25 lb test curve and fixed spool reel with 8 lb line. Equally a stout float or feeder rod will do the job. In all cases a hook of about size 8 or 10 will suffice for lip-hooking a typical chub bait of minnow, bleak or gudgeon. Such a set-up can be trotted through or alongside a likely looking swim such as those featuring overhanging bushes, bridge buttresses, sunken barges and banks undercut by the current. Alternatively a stalking approach can be used though if there are a lot of bushes, trees and general undergrowth to get through a shorter rod will be required. In both cases a stealthy approach, being quiet and staying out of sight of the fish, is needed as chub have a wholly justified reputation for disappearing the moment they spot an angler.

Another River Aire chub – 5 lb 13 oz – for Richard Young.

Here it is worth mentioning that when I was first thinking about the ideas for this book, Paul Gustafson, more well known for being a pike fisherman and author of *How to Catch Bigger Pike*, had just caught a 7 lb 3 oz specimen chub on livebait from the River Thames near Oxford. He had been observing the swim in question and seen fish to over 8 lb, taking this particular fish with a float-fished live minnow on a size 8 hook and 8 lb line. In fact, prior to actually fishing a good tip is to wander along the river early in the morning with some polarised glasses looking at the areas where the chub might be. This can save a lot of time and effort when the day comes to actually fishing for them.

Lure fishing for chub can also be an exhilarating way of catching them. To say the least, takes can be ferocious and the strength of the fight thrilling. An 8/9 ft lure rod, fixed spool reel with line of about 6 to 8 lb plus, of course, the lures are all that is needed. Most of my chub have been caught on Yorkshire rivers such as the Swale, Ure, Ouse and Derwent, though I have yet to catch a real specimen here using lures. This is not the case for Shaun Cunnane who also likes Yorkshire rivers for chub especially the Aire and Wharfe.

Shaun likes to target chub using lures at the beginning of the season, typically on the Aire near Skipton. He sets out with minimal tackle in the shape of 'some sort of short spinning rod, a fixed spool reel with 6 lb line and a box of small lures including Mepps spinners'. If the water is low an early start is best in order to find the feeding chub, this being done by flicking his spinner near to far bank hiding places under overhanging trees and bushes or alongside nearside bank reeds and weeds. Again the need for stealth has to be emphasised because the fish are very easily spooked.

Shaun points out that the older predatory chub will take lures without hesitation. The key is to land the lure where the chub are lying in wait and they will then find it hard to refuse what seems a free meal. They probably relish such a big meal and perhaps ignore baits which they have seen many times before; a lure is something different, perhaps something they do not usually associate with danger.

It is also worth mentioning that chub can be caught livebaiting by paternostering and ledgering baits and even by using small coarse deadbaits, though success tends to be harder especially with deadbaits. However, this did not prevent Danny Haynes, an angler more usually seen piking around the north-west of England, bagging up on chub on the River Wyre. He had found a likely looking chub holding swim on a slow flowing bend which featured a deeper hole beneath overhanging willow trees. Sure enough ledgered live minnows soon led to some fine chub around the 3 lb mark being caught, with one session producing over twenty fish. 'The action was really hectic at times' he was at pains to say about that particular day.

Trout

I now come to trout, *Salmo trutta*, and here, as previously, I refer to both brown trout and sea trout as taxonomically they are the same. Thus, although there are many local forms and varieties, as far as scientists are concerned there is only one natural trout in the British Isles namely brown and sea trout. Both are excellent sporting fish and though more usually seen as game fish and thus fished for by fly-fishing methods, they can be and are caught by more obviously predator fishing methods.

Brown trout spend their entire life in rivers or stillwaters, as distinct from sea trout which start life in freshwater but then later migrate to the sea. Both have similar general features, being streamlined with a blue-grey, olive-brown or black back, and silver or golden flanks with numerous red or brown spots mostly above the lateral line. The belly is white, silver or golden-yellow and there is a small dark red-orange adipose fin and thick 'wrist' at the base of the tail. The spawning females become darker while spawning males become reddish brown with a pronounced hook (kype) on the lower jaw. The first signs of difference occur as the sea trout prepare for the sea by changing to the silvery appearance of the smolt. When returning to freshwater they have blue-grey backs and silver flanks with black spots and a white belly. They breed with resident brown trout when the two come together on spawning grounds, this being unsurprising as the spawning process of both is identical.

Trout generally spawn between October and December in clean flowing water with gravel, though some stillwater fish do utilise wave-washed shorelines. The female excavates a depression (redd) by turning on her side and making vigorous undulating motions with her tail. Males sometimes fight to join a particular female before defending the redd from competitors. The female then lays her eggs in the redd where they are fertilised by the male and covered with gravel by the female's tail. This process may be repeated several times with the number of eggs laid dependent on the female's size, say, about 1800 per 2 lb.

Spawning takes place repeatedly over several years and trout can live to about 24 years. Sexual maturity is attained at two or three years and although they go under various stages of migration – some remain in their natal water, some move downstream or into stillwaters or even estuaries ('slob' trout) - they generally return to their natal water to spawn. Growth and size depends on genetic and environmental factors with 'ferox' trout of deep lakes, lochs and loughs, which prey entirely on fish, weighing up to over 30 lb. More usually the smaller trout feed on aquatic and terrestrial invertebrates and a brown trout from an upland stream or tarn may not even reach 1 lb. However, those living in rivers with ideal conditions can exceed 5 lb. On average, because they can exploit the rich feeding available in the sea, sea trout tend to be larger being on average between 3 and 10 lb but occasionally reaching over 20 lb.

Sea trout leave for the sea in spring as smolts at about two or three years of age, thereafter having a diet of crustaceans and fish such as herring or sandeels. Unlike salmon they stay fairly near their home rivers. Some, often known as whitling, return after only a few months at sea in July and August, others return after one to three years from April to August but also in the autumn on rivers such as the Tyne, Coquet and some Welsh rivers. Like salmon they return to their natal river but, unlike salmon, repeat spawning is common.

Trout are widely distributed throughout the British Isles though less so in East Anglia and the south-east of England because of unsuitable natural habitat, habitat degradation or poor quality water. In addition, sea trout are more common on the western coasts of the British Isles. In rivers trout require shallow, clean, well-oxygenated flowing water with mainly cobble or gravel substrates. They also prefer abundant cover provided by substrate, undercut banks and aquatic vegetation. Stillwaters that have similar characteristics are also to their liking. The older fish prefer deeper water to which fry may also migrate in winter. They also require unimpeded access to their spawning grounds and sea trout in particular, because of their generally larger size and more extensive movements over the length of the river also require holding areas to provide refuges on their migration upstream.

As for fishing for trout, as Colin Willock notes in *The New ABC of Fishing*, 'it is customary to assert that the only sporting way of catching trout is with a fly' (p 224) which also includes small lures that resemble fish fry. Such a view may be rather outdated or one more common amongst game anglers and die-hard fly-fishers in particular, but it surely goes without saying that many, including regular freshwater predator anglers, might disagree. Having said that, there is no doubt that fly-fishing is a very skilful, successful technique, this being evidenced by the fact that it has been taken up by some pike anglers in search of their quarry. Perhaps there remains an element of snobbishness in some fly-fishing circles but I do not want to go into a lengthy discussion about this other than to repeat that fly-fishing – wet and dry fly, dapping and the like – is a very good way of catching trout, both brown and sea. At the risk of being overly brief, the correct tackle needs to be used not least matching rod and line (floating and sinking), leaders, reel, backing line, dry and wet flies and accessories such as landing net, knife, forceps and the like. Typically then the rod will be about 9 ft with a tapered leader ending with, say, 3 or 4 lb line. As for flies, good 'all-rounders', both wet and dry, include Coachman, Pheasant Tail and Gold Ribbed Hare's Ear.

My nephew, Adam, was, and to some extent still is, a keen trout fly-fisher having fished with success on waters as varied as Yorkshire's River Wharfe, Northumberland's River Till and on lochs in the south-west of Scotland. Whether using a wet or dry fly, if at all possible he likes to wade out into the water and then cast up and across the river. The fly then fishes in a wide arc and if the current and flow is right you can, for example, allow it to drift under bushes or trees on the far bank where the trout are likely to be. He particularly likes to use dry flies in sunnier conditions when the trout are likely to be hooked as soon as the fly touches the water; it is almost as if the trout rises and takes the fly spontaneously.

When it comes to dapping, which is particularly popular in Ireland and Scotland, it is usually carried out from a boat. A far longer rod is used, from about 14 to 18 ft long, as are live flies such as the mayfly and daddy longlegs, though artificial ones resembling the same also have their day.

In passing, it must be said that although fly-fishing and dapping for sea trout involves much the same as for brown trout there is an important exception. This is the

Adam Rogowski with a brace of River Wharfe trout.

fact that more experienced sea trout anglers often fish throughout the night simply because it can be more productive. Suffice to say it is more difficult, not least because of having to cast in the dark, and so is not really recommended for the uninitiated.

Despite the above, many use other methods to catch trout. Indeed probably the easiest way to catch them is to use ordinary coarse fishing methods such as float or ledgered baits like maggots and worms. If a river or stillwater has recently been stocked then such fishing can be very successful even to the extent of the angler thinking that trout are simply too easy to catch. It is partly because of this that others, including myself, prefer to use spinning and baitfishing methods.

A younger Steve Rogowski with two nice River Wharfe trout.

Despite those fly-fishers who think that spinning for trout is also too easy and is, in effect, cheating, it really can be an exciting way to fish for them. Tackle consists of a light 7 or 8 ft spinning rod with a matching fixed spool reel and monofilament line of about 5 lb. You can use fresh minnows if you want although they are a bit soft and do not survive a lot of casting. As a result I have found small Mepps or Mepps-like spinners to be very effective though one would be unwise to neglect spoons and plugs. In flowing water, cast downstream and retrieve varying the speed and searching holding places like holes, banks of vegetation, furrows and so on. Upstream fishing can also be done but is more difficult because the current affects the movement of the lure. On stillwaters again it is a matter of casting and retrieving perhaps in a fan-like fashion thereby ensuring that all the water is covered in each swim. All takes can be breathtaking, as can be the subsequent fight, with fish of only 1 lb or so putting up an excellent, tail-leaping scrap.

Spinning, of course, involves the use of lures and if you are going to target the really big 'ferox' trout of large stillwaters then one of the best ways of doing this is by trolling which, simply put, means pulling a lure, or a bait for that matter, behind a boat. The large lochs and loughs of Scotland and Ireland, as well as some of the larger lakes in the English Lake District are some of the waters to target. For example, as he pointed out in *Pike Fishing in the UK and Ireland* (edited by the author) Stephen Hincks spends much of his fishing in the Lake District targeting pike which in turn often involves trolling for them. He also points out that trout up to about 16 lb can be caught in the process. For such fishing strong tackle, not least rod, reel and line are required. He also advises that it is not just a matter of chucking out a couple of lures and then motoring off down the lake. Rather, a more methodical method is used namely picking out a depth band and sticking to it until success is found. As far as 'ferox' trout are concerned he reckons using a deep trolling lure over, not surprisingly, deep water is a good tip.

Stephen Hincks with a lovely English Lakeland ferox trout which took a whole mackerel meant for pike.

I have mentioned using dead minnows in terms of spinning for trout but they, along with other small fish like gudgeon, can also be used as livebaits. All that is needed is a light rod and reel capable of holding line again of about 5 lb, a float and a size 8 hook. Then all you have to do is to lip-hook the bait and gently cast into a likely looking swim. The bait will do its work, as will the flow of the river, until hopefully it is grabbed by a hungry 'brownie' with the fight and fun then beginning. While I am on the subject, livebaits can also be ledgered and, I guess, paternostered but overall I much prefer to see the sight of a bobbing free roving/roaming or trotted float; to coin a popular phrase it really is pleasing on the eye.

You can also, as suggested, catch trout using coarse and sea deadbaits although it has to be said that it can be very slow. Nevertheless, again Stephen Hincks has had 'ferox' trout on such as whole mackerel and I once caught a nice 3 lb brownie on a dead gudgeon on Lake Coniston. Regarding the latter, a mate, Mark Goddard, and I had been piking with deadbaits all day long without as much as a sniff of a run. Suddenly though there was a hesitant bleep from one of the bite alarms and the drop-back, yes, dropped back. I quickly struck and immediately knew I had hooked a fish but could tell it was not a pike because of the way it fought. What a surprise it was when we eventually saw the beautifully marked brown trout in the net. It also really made the day for us both because otherwise a blank would have occurred.

Salmon

I now come to what for many is the 'King of Fishes', namely the Atlantic salmon, *Salmo salar*. They really are magnificent, hard-fighting fish that are the game angler's dream and therefore, as with trout, fly-fishing comes into its own along with such as worming. But again more obvious predator angling methods like spinning and bait-fishing come into play.

The salmon is the only native salmon in the British Isles being widely distributed in northern and south-western England, Wales, Scotland and Ireland. They are also found in the chalk streams of southern England. However, they are threatened by such as pollution and over-exploitation and, like trout, are absent from East Anglia and large areas of central and southern England. Other factors in relation to their absence from the latter areas are unsuitable natural habitat, habitat degradation, poor water quality and obstructions to the natural passages of fish in rivers.

Salmon in some ways resemble trout. They are streamlined with a small, dark adipose fin and narrow 'wrist' at the base of the tail. The back is blue-grey, flanks silver with black spots mostly above the lateral line, and the belly is white. Spawning females (hens) are darker in colour with the spawning males (cocks) being reddish brown with a pronounced hook (kype) on the lower jaw. However, parr (juveniles) are brownish with dark markings along the flanks and spotted black, brown and red, while prior to migrating to the sea, the smolts become silvery.

When it comes to biology, behaviour and habitat again the similarities with trout become apparent. Spawning is virtually the same apart from the fact that a mature parr may dart in the redd and fertilise the eggs before the male gets a chance. In addition, spawning occurs between October and January but usually in November and December. The resultant parr are territorial and feed on aquatic and terrestrial invertebrates before, after between one and three years, they journey to the sea as smolts after which they then prefer zoo plankton and fish such as capelin and sandeels. They remain at sea between one and three years, feeding in the North Atlantic around Greenland and the Faroe Islands before returning in the spring. If they return after one year they are on their maiden spawning run and are known as grilse. They have a strong homing instinct and as a result the majority return to spawn in the river in which they hatched, fighting their way upstream with every surge of rainwater. They can grow large with, for example, the British record being a fish well over 60 lb though those in the 8 to 15 lb bracket are regarded a decent size.

Some rivers have a run of fresh fish virtually every month, while others have a bias towards a spring or autumn run, though sometimes there is a summer run as well. All this usually only takes place once even though after spawning they try to get back to sea; at this stage they are emaciated, even eel-like, in their appearance and called kelts. In passing, I once caught a 4 lb kelt on a paternostered live skimmer bream while piking on the Yorkshire Ouse. While it put up a worthwhile scrap I did feel rather sorry about the scrawny state it was in. In fact, most do not make the sea and die trying to get there, this being because reaching the spawning grounds and spawning itself takes a lot out of them, and they also appear to eat very little, if at all, when back in freshwater.

This 4 lb salmon kelt for Steve Rogowski took a paternostered live skimmer bream meant for pike on the River Ouse.

Young salmon, again like trout, require shallow, clean, well oxygenated and fast flowing waters with gravel and cobble substrate, together with lots of cover in the form of such as substrate and undercut banks. While the younger parr are well adapted to swimming in riffles, older parr often prefer deeper water. Adult salmon also require access to their spawning grounds and to holding areas which then provide refuge on their migration up the river.

Repeating an earlier comment, salmon do not generally eat in the river. They are often torpid and live off their sea fat but for some reason they do snap at the angler's offering. Perhaps it is because they retain their biting instinct or because they need to fight for resting and holding places, chasing other fish away and consequently taking the angler's offering. Whatever the reason, those wanting to fish for salmon will have to put up with similar comments made in relation to trout, namely that the only real way to catch them is by fly-fishing. But again as with trout many predator anglers, while acknowledging that fly-fishing is skilful and a successful method of catching them, would rather spin or bait fish for them or even use methods such as worming and prawning/shrimping. Here I briefly look at these methods in turn.

For fly-fishing one requires similar, if stepped up, tackle as is used for trout. For example, a rod of 12 to 15 ft, suitable reel, sinking line, a leader of about 12 lb and larger flies, some with treble as opposed to single hooks. Dry flies can be used though wet flies predominate, with classic examples of salmon flies being Thunder and Lightning, Jock Stotts, Hairy Mairy and Allys Shrimp. As for worming and prawning/ shrimping, a salmon or pike rod of 11 or 12 ft with a fixed spool reel holding 14 lb monofilament line ought to suffice, together with drilled bullets. The lobworms or prawn/shrimp are then mounted on large, say 4 or 6 hooks and are simply left to trundle along the river bed, though in Ireland the use of a float is more common.

For spinning and even baitfishing a strong lure/spinning rod of 10/11 ft with a fixed spool or multiplying reel with 10 to 12 lb monofilament line is needed. Devon Minnows of about 3 to 4 inches are standard lures for the spring while for later in the year spoons including Tobies and Mepps/Mepps-like spinners like Flying Condoms can be very effective. Floating and sinking plugs can also be used. Overall perhaps as rule of thumb dull coloured spoons and devons do best in low water, dark brown/black with a gold belly is useful in summer, and in spring all silver is preferable. And when it comes to actually fishing such artificials one could do worse, especially in spring, than re-member the old adage: 'Fish down and across, fish deep, fish slow'. Of course, as with all fishing, this should not prevent one from, in effect, throwing the rule book away and experimenting or 'ringing the changes' whenever possible.

As for baitfishing, which essentially amounts to spinning with a natural bait, then a number of baits can be used. I have already referred to worms and prawns/shrimps, but in the past preserved sprats, eel tails and herring were popular baits in the spring though are less used these days. Later in the year minnows and sandeels come into their own. It is worth noting that salmon still feed on sandeels both along the coast and in estuaries so in brackish water a live lip-hooked sandeel will catch. Bass can also be

Mike and Adam Rogowski spinning for salmon on the River Till.

attracted though for many of us this is no bad thing.

For all salmon fishing, indeed fishing more generally, the key to success is knowing where the fish are likely to be and fortunately in many ways they are predictable creatures. When on the move they are virtually uncatchable so it is resting places or holding pools that should be looked for. They like stones and boulders, since sand and mud irritate their gills, so when these form quiet, deep pools out of the main current they should be the angler's target. In flood conditions, before they have taken up their lies, the fish can be expected almost anywhere but especially in the broad, shallow tails of big pools. But the mention of stones and boulders reminds me of my nephew Adam catching his first salmon and in what follows he describes what happened.

Despite being an avid reader of *Trout and Salmon* magazine, albeit mainly for the trout fishing content, and also having read Hugh Falkus' famous tome *Salmon Fishing*, I could in no way claim to be an experienced salmon fisher. Indeed, despite several trips to south-west Scotland's River Annan I have yet to catch one there.

37

However, the capture of my first salmon from the River Bladnoch, also in south-west Scotland, surely demonstrates that the average angler, given the right conditions and applying watercraft gleaned from predator angling more generally, can catch the 'King of Fishes'.

My view is that there are at least two important factors to bear in mind when salmon fishing. First, and not surprisingly, there is location. While pike like to ambush prey from such as a weedbed sanctuary, things are different for salmon. Although they do not feed in freshwater they will grab at the angler's lure as they surge upstream, this being particularly so from, for instance, a pool of deep slack water behind a boulder. Second, there is the choice of lure. I am a firm believer that confidence is the key to a great deal of fishing and when it comes to lures for salmon I prefer something along the lines of a rotating, flashing blade which incorporates a wriggling skirt. Invariably then, for me it is a Flying Condom that inspires confidence.

So we come to the capture of my fish. I had been working a stretch of the River Bladnoch near Newton Stewart but unfortunately with no sign of any salmon. River conditions looked the part being a little above normal but going down. I remained quietly confident especially on coming across what I thought looked a likely holding pool; a deep slack of water behind a large, mid-stream boulder. The red 'condom' was flicked to the far side of the slack and worked back across the river. There only seemed to be a couple of cranks of the reel before a fresh-run fish rolled on the lure and was, as it turned out, firmly hooked. Remembering what I had read, I resisted the temptation to try and land it as quickly as possible so as not to lose it. Instead the fish was allowed to set the pace as it went on a blistering run down two pools, while I looked for a place to land it when it started to tire. Eventually, some ten minutes later, I managed to grip it by the tail and lift it out of the water with the weighing revealing a fine 9 lb fish. It really is no wonder that to this day the capture of this fish remains one of the highlights of my angling career.

In my view, Adam does manage to convey the thrills involved in catching what for many remains the ultimate sporting fish.

Themes and Organisation of the Book

Recapping a little, so far I have covered the attractions of freshwater predator fishing, followed by the rationale for choosing the particular species that form the bulk of this book, namely pike, catfish, eels, perch and zander. I have also briefly looked at these species. Thereafter I turned to chub, trout and salmon, all of which can be caught by using predator fishing methods even though they are not generally targeted by freshwater predator anglers. At this point then it is timely to turn to the general themes and organisation of the book itself. Obviously, it is about fishing for pike and freshwater predator fish in the British Isles, with the main species being dealt with in chapters two to six while chapter seven provides some concluding thoughts.

Adam Rogowski with his first salmon, weighing 9 lb from south-west Scotland's River Bladnoch; a Flying Condom lure did the trick.

In chapter two I deal with pike fishing, the pike being the largest and certainly one of the most common native freshwater predators of the British Isles. I begin by looking at the various types of waters that contain these supreme predators, together with locating them on these waters. Then I turn to my favourite methods of angling for them, namely baitfishing from the bank using lives and deads. And it is worth remembering that despite the growth of boat and lure fishing they remain the most popular. But boat fishing with these methods as well as lure and fly-fishing are not forgotten and are also discussed. In so doing, tackle and equipment, baits and lures, including flies, are covered. All this is interspersed with some interesting pike fishing stories.

Simon Clarke looks at the catfish itself and catfishing in particular in chapter three. He begins with such as the catfish's biology, behaviour and distribution. Being an introduced species it is not as widespread as most of the other freshwater predators featured in this book but even so it is within reasonable reach of many anglers, especially those in southern Britain. When it comes to fishing for them, Simon deals with, for instance, waters, bait, tackle, methods and rigs, and hooking, playing and landing a catfish. He also recalls catching his first catfish and other memorable captures.

Eels feature in chapter four written by Steve Ormrod. One of the major concerns these days is about the eel's dramatic decline, something which Steve comments upon while acknowledging that steps are being taken to address this. He begins though by describing the eel's strange and fascinating life cycle before dealing with such as location and habitats, tackle, tactics, baits and rigs, and hooking, playing and handling large eels. There is also a very interesting account of his (unfortunately losing) battle with a large eel.

Mark Barrett writes about one of his favourite species, the handsome but greedy perch in chapter five. His keenness on the fish is evidenced in that he has actually kept some at home in aquariums this helping him to get a better understanding of their lives and behaviour. Indeed, he begins with a look at perch lives and habitat along with their distribution, before moving to locating them and when to actually go fishing for them. Tackle and bait, including using artificials/lures, methods and some memorable perch fishing days are also recounted.

Chapter six features Neville Fickling's contribution on zander and fishing for them. He bemoans the unauthorised spread of the species, however, because of the damage it can do to pike stocks though acknowledges that he likes them and that they are a fascinating fish for the angler to target. Biology and behaviour are dealt with before water conditions, when to go fishing for them and location are considered. After tackle, bait and methods, he recalls some memorable zander sessions before ending with a brief guide to zander waters and a look at the new zander record.

Finally, in chapter seven I look at some current challenges and future prospects in relation to pike and freshwater predator fishing in the British Isles. The challenges dealt with relate to the decline of the eel, global warming and climate change, anti-angling and what I refer to as miscellaneous challenges such as the illegal capture and eating of freshwater fish including predators, invasive species and pollution. Finally, and as stated earlier, in looking at future prospects, and despite the challenges, an optimistic view is taken of the future.

Conclusion

All in all then, this book has something important and interesting to say to all those attracted to pike and freshwater predator fishing in the British Isles. This is the case whether they are simply contemplating taking up the sport, beginners to it or are more experienced anglers. All such readers will, I am sure, find something that will capture and hold their attention. This could be the discussions of the fish species themselves and the many and varied waters that contain them. It could be advice and guidance on such as tackle, methods, rigs and baits. And last, but certainly not least, it could be reading about some memorable pike and freshwater predator fishing catches.

2
Pike
Steve Rogowski

As the pike, *Esox lucius*, is the British Isles' largest native freshwater predator fish it is not surprising that it is the source of many myths and legends. Often it is almost impossible to verify the truth or otherwise of these stories, something which Neville Fickling acknowledges in *Mammoth Pike*. For instance, there is the 90 lb 8 oz fish from Lough Derg in 1862 and the 72 lb fish from Loch Ken in1774. Neville includes them in his list of 35 lb plus rod-caught pike though acknowledges doubts about their authenticity. Then there is possibly the most famous pike of all, the Endrick pike of 1934. It was found dead at the mouth of the River Endrick as it enters Loch Lomond and was said to have weighed 70 lb. All such fish, and it goes without saying there are quite a few others, have their doubters and many would even pour scorn on such stories.

In truth, apart from the 50 lb fish found dead in 1995 at The Warren, Essex, pike generally only grow to the 40 lb plus mark. Thus, we have Roy Lewis' 46 lb 13 oz lure-caught fish from Llandegfedd Reservoir in 1992, with other authenticated examples being the again lure-caught Lough Mask pike of 42 lb caught by Ottoman Airing and Bert Rozemeijer in 1996 and 1995 respectively. Into the new millennium we have such as Martin Godfrey's 41 lb 12 oz pike caught on a live trout at Bewl Water in 2000 and Eric Edwards' 41 lb 8 oz fish caught on a lure from Blithfield Reservoir in 2001. In 2004 Lough Mask again produced the goods with a 40 lb fish for Russell Taylor on a fly. And in 2007 Derek MacDonald caught a 41 lb fish but as I write all we know is that it came from a trout reservoir on 'a large bait suspended under a drifter float'. It must be stressed that such 40 lb plus fish are very rare and although 30 lb fish are caught every year, the big thirties, of over 35 lb are again almost equally uncommon. And even 30 lb fish are beyond the reach of many pike anglers. Naturally these facts do not stop many of us continuing to try, and in any case one has only to recall that even smaller fish certainly test your gear and angling skills.

This chapter begins with a discussion of pike waters and the location of pike. After all to catch them you have to know where they are likely to be. Second, I look at bait-fishing from the bank, including tackle, methods, techniques and baits; despite the increase in boat and lure fishing, this is still the most popular form of pike fishing. Third, I deal with baitfishing from a boat and include boats themselves and equipment, tackle and methods and techniques. Fourth, I turn to lure fishing, including fly-fishing, both from the bank and boat; this includes tackle together with the lures and flies themselves and ways of using them.

Pike Waters and Location

If one ignores the rather blatant advertising at times, the *Fox Guide to Modern Pike Fishing* provides a useful introduction to pike fishing and in particular, pike waters. Hence, pike are to be found in a wide variety of waters throughout the British Isles with the exception of northernmost Scotland, most of the offshore islands and many upland areas elsewhere. These pike-holding waters range from ponds, drains and canals to rivers, lakes, pits and reservoirs. I begin this section with rivers, reservoirs and lakes, these being the waters I am most familiar with, prior to looking at canals and drains, and gravel and clay pits.

Rivers

I love pike fishing on rivers especially those in Yorkshire such as the Swale, Ure, Aire Derwent and, not least, the Ouse. All rivers, including these Yorkshire ones, have a character and personality of their own with such as pacey, weedy swims then giving way to deep, ox-bow bends with overhanging willows. Pike, with their streamlined bodies, are perfectly equipped to cope with all such changes including strong currents, though admittedly you will usually find them in the slacker waters.

Rivers start with steep gradients and narrow, boulder and cobble strewn valleys where trout predominate. As the gradient eases, the current slows, and sand and gravel appear as do fish such as grayling. The gradient then eases further while the volume of water increases from the input of tributaries, and weed and other vegetation appears, as do coarse fish more generally like chub, barbel, roach, dace, perch and pike. Finally in the lowest reaches, the river meanders over a wide floodplain where coarse fish predominate along with migratory fish like salmon, lampreys and eels. Of course there is no abrupt change in these zones and some rivers, such as the chalk streams of southern England and short Scottish Highland rivers, do not follow this zonation. River engineering, for navigation, power or flood defence for example, can also influence the natural patterns of these zones. The Fen rivers, for instance, are very slow flowing, soft-bottomed and often coloured as dykes and side drains pump excess water into them. These conditions can actually be productive as I well recall from one of my first visits to the Great Ouse.

I arrived soon after first light on a grey, chilly February day and the Ouse, along with the adjoining tributary, looked extremely coloured. You could even be forgiven for thinking that the pike would have been totally put off feeding. Nevertheless the rods were quickly set up and cast and it was not long before a mackerel tail was snaffled by a 5 lb 8 oz fish which gave a decent account of itself. This was soon followed by a nice

43

A nice Great Ouse River pike for Steve Rogowski.

Checking a run soon after dawn on Steve Rogowski's favourite river swim, also on the Ouse but this time in Yorkshire.

12 lb 8 oz, this also falling to a mackerel tail. Thereafter, apart from a brief lull in the early afternoon, the action continued as pike kept coming to the net or I missed the runs. They were not massive fish, the largest being a 15 lb 8 oz that took a liking to a dead chub, but at times the activity was quite hectic and by the end of the session a total of twelve pike for 98 lb were landed.

Most areas of the British Isles have rivers containing pike. I have already mentioned some of the Yorkshire ones and the Great Ouse, and England also has such as the Avon and Thames in the south, the Severn and Wye in the west, and the Thurne in the east. The Severn and Wye actually originate in central Wales and the latter country also has such as the Dee in the north. Scotland's rivers, such as the Tay and Spey, are more renowned for their game fishing though they do contain pike, albeit access can often be difficult. Finally, Ireland has such as the mighty Shannon and the Suck. I well remember a recent visit to the latter when the river was quite swollen after heavy rain and conditions were generally less than ideal. However, luckily I managed to find a deep, slower moving slack within easy casting distance. Sure enough within half an hour of casting I was into and landed a hard-fighting double. Several more pike were caught and all were into double figures, so it really was a decent session.

As with all piking, location is the key to success on rivers so a mobile approach is often recommended, by leap-frogging the rods through several swims, for example. Other than this, target features like weirs, bridges, where tributaries/side streams enter, much as I did on the Great Ouse, and snags. Weirs are well oxygenated which pike love especially in summer, but can be very snaggy with resulting tackle losses so it is best to step up the strength of line/braid, traces, hooks and the like, as well as proceeding with an element of caution. On the other hand, bridges offer shelter to prey and hence attract pike, sometimes in large numbers. Where tributaries/side streams enter rivers, deeper slacks and pools are formed these providing great ambush areas for pike. Finally, when I refer to snags this means virtually any obstruction such as large boulders, islands, sunken/overhanging trees and bushes, weedbeds, sunken barges, and even islands. They all provide shelter for prey and not far behind you will usually find the pike.

A problem with river piking, increasingly so over recent years it seems, is winter flooding which means that often rivers are almost unfishable. I am only too well aware of this from my many sessions on the Yorkshire Ouse. At such times pike take to side streams and backwaters like marinas in order to get out of the main flow, so these are good areas to try. Flooded cattle drinks and slack water around locks or bridges are another good feature to target.

Reservoirs

Reservoirs are important as far as pike fishing is concerned. Coarse fish like roach, perch and bream mean the pike are not usually short of food, and when trout are stocked regularly some really big pike can appear. One has only to recall such as Llandegfedd in South Wales and Blithfield in the midlands of England. Such

This 20 lb 6 oz reservoir pike took a ledgered dead roach for Steve Rogowski.

reservoirs can be prolific in terms of numbers and size of pike, but equally others can be very daunting and prove to be very hard to crack. This is so on many of the reservoirs I am most familiar with in the north-west of England. On a cold, grey winter's day you are often left wondering if the rods are near any pike at all. If you persevere though, putting in the time and effort, it can bring rewards.

I well remember one December tackling a northern reservoir next to the valve tower near the dam wall. As winter approached, I had moved to the deeper water and was enjoying, if largely blanking, in the short daytime sessions. On this particular grey, if mild day, the rods had barely been in for half an hour when the alarm screamed away as the mackerel tail had done the trick and a fine chunky specimen, which went to 27 lb 8 oz, was quickly netted. As a result, over the last few years I have always gravitated back to this swim as November and December approached, but with only the odd jack being caught. During 2007 after thirteen blanks even the jacks had deserted me. However, on the fourteenth visit on a grey, drizzly but again mild day I tried ledgering a rainbow trout tail, strangely a bait I had never used before. All was quiet until dusk approached when the drop-back shuddered and the alarm bleeped hesitantly. On striking I soon knew I was into a solid fish as it hugged the bottom. She gradually surfaced before, after a head shake and an attempted tail-walk, she was in the net; 'another chunky specimen, at last' I thought to myself with the weighing revealing her to be 24 lb 6 oz.

Reservoirs vary a lot in size from tens of acres to hundreds and even thousands of acres in the case of Rutland Water. The smaller ones can be less daunting but on all reservoirs locating features, both above and below the surface, helps locate the pike. This is easier said than done on the concrete bowl type reservoirs, for example the four hundred acre Cheddar Reservoir in Somerset or the much smaller Barrowford Reservoir near Colne which I am familiar with. At such waters often all you can do is cast the baits on the gradients around the edge and hope for the best, or try and locate the pike by using lures. Luckily most reservoirs do have some features and are therefore easier to tackle.

The most obvious features are, of course, those above the water and which can be simply seen. Most have a dam wall at one end and this can be a good area to try. Algae will be there and hence prey fish, and the wall itself will provide cover for pike. In winter pike are attracted because of the deep water at the dam end because of the resulting temperature and water stability. Similar comments regarding algae and prey fish apply to valve towers or old pump houses that are also often to be found.

On trout reservoirs floating trout cages mean that the trout therein will be regularly fed so other fish are attracted to the free food as well as in turn the pike. Other surface features that are often present include such as inlets and streams, overhanging bushes and trees, and weed and reed beds. All provide

Steve Rogowski with a 24 lb 6 oz reservoir pike which snaffled a ledgered rainbow trout tail at dusk.

47

Visiting reservoirs when the water is down reveals features such as shelves, channels and drop-offs.

cover and/or food for prey fish, this in itself attracting pike as well as the fact that all such features provide good ambush points.

When it comes to features under the surface, as reservoirs are generally formed by damming a valley, they can be many and varied. There may be old tracks/roads, buildings, walls, fences, trees, piles of rubble, drop-offs, troughs, river/stream beds and so on. All these break up the water and hence attract prey fish and pike. It is stating the obvious but the best way to find such features, other than gaining local knowledge by asking, is to visit the reservoir in summer when the water will be well down. By making a mental note, or better still written and/or photographic notes you will be able to locate them precisely and then be ready for the autumn/winter campaign.

Lakes

By lakes I refer to a range of stillwaters from small human-made ponds or lakes of under an acre to the huge glacial lakes, lochs and loughs which are miles long and wide. Examples of the latter include Lake Windermere in the English Lake District, Lochs

Lomond and Awe in Scotland, Bala Lake (or Llyn Tegid) in Wales, and Loughs Mask and Corrib in Ireland. All these varying lakes, from small to huge, and every size in between, are amongst the most popular types of water for catching pike. Indeed, although they can be prolific in terms of the smaller fish, they also contain pike over the thirty and even forty pound mark.

Smaller, shallower waters, such as estate lakes and meres, can be a challenge but they are usually easier than the larger waters simply because there is less water for the pike to swim in so your rods have a better chance of being near some fish. Again features are the key to location such as natural marginal cover like weed and reed beds, bushes and trees. As a result distance casting is usually unnecessary, as a gentle flick of the bait to such features is all that is needed. Other good features to try include points and islands as these may well be patrol points for pike.

When it comes to the larger waters, say over a hundred acres or so, then it does mean that success can be harder. Where do you start when the water can be hundreds of feet deep and so large that they can often seem like inland seas? My key bit of advice would be to mentally divide the lake up into several smaller sections and target these one at a time. Target the features, both surface and sub-surface as mentioned above, and eventually the water and pike fishing will reveal itself. Naturally, the use of a boat with such as sonar will make things easier and help you find other features such as deep basins, rocks, underwater reefs and plateaus. When you feel you know a particular section, move on to the next until the whole lake is covered.

A moody Lough Mask and Steve Rogowski's rods are in.

49

I found Lake Windermere a challenge when I first considered piking escapades to this famous water. Gaining access from the bank can be a problem as much of it is in private hands, and even when you can get to the water casting can be difficult because of the trees right on the shoreline and even wading out is not always the answer as the bank shelves away very quickly. All this did not stop me persevering though and eventually I had success on a warm, sunny April day. I was in an area that has weedbeds a couple of rod lengths out in summer, followed by deeper water to about fifteen feet as the shelf deepens away. After the rods were cast, there turned out to be a three hour

Steve Rogowski caught this 17 lb Windermere pike on a ledgered lamprey section.

A summer's daybreak on Windermere, and a contemplative 'Spinning' Steve Appleby.

wait before there was a couple of bleeps from one of the bite alarms. Initially I thought an inquisitive swan was the culprit as it paddled about near my line, but the alarm suddenly went ballistic and on winding down and striking I soon knew I was into a nice fish. She stayed on the bottom for a while before surfacing with a bit of a tail-walk, and after a couple of sizzling runs she was in the net and weighed in at exactly 17 lb; 'what a way to crack Windy!' I remember saying to myself. The action was not over by any means though and not too long afterwards two alarms were triggered in the space of five minutes leading to decent fish of 10 lb and 13 lb. Thereafter I was having a bit of a celebratory doze, and probably dreaming of things pikey, when an alarm suddenly went off and I jumped to my feet, promptly falling over and cutting my lip quite badly in the process. This did not stop me striking home though, and after another tail-walking tussle a fine 15 lb was netted. Four decent fish for 55 lb is certainly not a bad session on what can be after all a hard water particularly from the bank.

A difference when tackling these large lakes is that occasionally, in high summer for instance, the pike can be found in open, featureless areas as they go searching for oxygenated water as the shallower water warms up. Also in summer they can sometimes be found suspended in mid-water. Alternatively in winter they can usually be found in deep water as the temperature drops.

Canals and Drains

Turning to canals and drains, these man-made waterways criss-cross various areas of England in particular. The obvious difference between them is that canals were built to transport goods before the advent of railways and modern roads, while drains were constructed to drain waterlogged land so as to prevent flooding and reclaim farmland. Both tend to be relatively shallow but other than this come in various sizes, with canals being generally narrow to suit barges, while drains can range from very narrow to huge channels.

Most canals are to be found in the old industrial areas of the north and midlands of England and they have only recently been restored and renovated. Perhaps one of the best known for pike fishing is the Bridgewater Canal in the north-west of England. They are also to be found in the other countries of the British Isles. For instance in Scotland there ares the Union, Forth-Clyde and Caledonian canals, while Ireland has such as the Grand Canal, and Wales the Llangollen Canal.

Dawn on an East Yorkshire canal.

Danny Haynes and a 16 lb 12 oz canal pike.

Overall drains are less common and are found in more specific areas. By far the most well known system is to be found in the Fens, an area of low, flat land which covers Cambridgeshire, south Lincolnshire and western Norfolk. This area has famous rivers such as the Great Ouse and Nene, but the drains are equally well known with examples being the Middle Level, Sixteen Foot, Twenty Foot and the Relief Channel. In the west of England there is another notable drain system, the Somerset Levels. Finally, in Kent waterways were built for drainage as well as for transport through the marshes.

Canals and drains generally have good access to the banks and can provide some comfortable piking. Drains in particular have to be dredged regularly so the banks tend to be devoid of such as trees and bushes. If the fishing is easy, it has to be said that, apart from the occasional Fenland thirty, the pike tend to be on the smaller side. Having said this, surprises do turn up from time to time as evidenced by a 37 lb 7 oz fish for Richard Cole from the Gloucester Canal in 2004.

As canals and drains tend to be mostly straight and featureless, locating the pike can be difficult. This means that the leap-frogging approach mentioned in relation to rivers can help, as can using lures by which a large area can be covered until the pike are found. Any features that do occur such as bridges, reed or weedbeds, and even the slightest bend or odd tree or bush on those featureless drains should also be thoroughly explored. On canals, lock gates attract prey fish and hence pike, as do inlets from/to small marinas where barges are moored. Prey fish often shoal up here during the winter in preparation for spawning; catch these areas right and the sport can be good as Danny Haynes and I have recently found when tackling a small canal in East Yorkshire. Lots of pike have been caught here and what is more they all tended to be doubles up to about the seventeen pound mark though surely a twenty awaits us. Finally, on both drains and canals, casting to the near and far margins more generally can often produce the goods as this is where pike tend to hold up.

Gravel and Clay Pits

Gravel and clay pits have only relatively recently appeared as they were excavated for materials used in such as the construction industry. The richest seams of gravel are along river valleys and their flood plains especially in the midlands, eastern and southern counties of England. Beneath the gravel, clay is usually found and clay pits are excavated deeper so generally they are not as rich and productive as gravel pits. Incidentally, gravel and clay pits are less common in the north and west as such areas tend to be quarried more for stone. Consequently the most notable pits are found along

Bill Palmer cradles a long 21 lb gravel pit pike.

the valleys of such as the Thames, Trent, Great Ouse, Wensum and Hampshire Avon. They vary enormously in size from a mere few acres to hundreds of acres, and increase in numbers each year.

Pits soon fill naturally with water and can become excellent settings for a variety of aquatic life. Some can then become picturesque while others seemingly remain as boring holes with water in them, though they are simply at different stages of development. As soon as fish appear, either naturally or by being stocked, the subsequent piking potential can be very good. Location though, as always, is the key.

Lures are a good way to get to know a pit and the piking hotspots. Good old-fashioned plumbing can also help find features such as troughs, drop-offs and localised holes. Slopes along gravel bars and the deeper margins around islands are also worth trying, as are the usual features like overhanging trees and bushes, weed and reedbeds. For instance, I well recall my first visit to a Fenland pit alongside the Great Ouse, and casting to a deeper trough which had overhanging trees/bushes soon led to some pike action even though I was actually targeting zander.

So, after briefly looking at the various types of pike waters, and at locating the pike in them, it is timely to turn to actually catching them, beginning with baitfishing from the bank.

Baitfishing from the Bank

As Barrie Rickards and Malcolm Bannister note in *The Great Modern Pike Anglers*, baitfishing for pike has come a long way over the last fifty years. No longer is such angling limited to short, stiff rods suspending a livebait under a large bung. Deadbaiting became more accepted in the 1960s and thereafter grew rapidly while tackle also improved with such as longer more flexible glass and carbon fibre rods replacing their less forgiving forebears. Tackle developments over subsequent decades were fast and furious – specialist floats, weigh slings, landing nets, bite alarms, further rod and reel improvements and so on – leading to the vast array of tackle that one sees today. Furthermore, deadbaiting has now overtaken livebaiting as the most popular method of catching pike. What tackle then do you need for these two excellent pike catching methods?

Tackle

As far as tackle is concerned, the first thing to consider is, unsurprisingly, the rod. You can get them for every conceivable piking situation from fishing on small rivers and drains to large reservoirs and lakes. Then there is the size of bait to consider, or the time of year. For example, arguably a different rod is needed to cast a small livebait as compared to a large deadbait, or in winter a pike may swim quite willingly to the net whereas in summer they fight much harder so again a different rod may be required. However, a word of caution, as the number of different rods on offer are often more designed to separate an angler from his hard-earned money than put more fish on the bank. My view is that you can get away with two types of rod for bank fishing namely, for short-medium range fishing, an 11 ft rod with a 2.5 to 3 lb test curve, and for long range fishing a 12 ft rod with a 3 to 4 lb test curve, though for drifter float fishing a 13 ft version may be needed. Such rods will enable you to deal with every conceivable situation with confidence, from casting different bait sizes at short and long range to piking in snag-free or snaggy water.

The second important bit of tackle is, again unsurprisingly, the reel. These days for bank fishing a good quality fixed spool reel is required. As with rods, there are many on the market but in essence you need ones that are rugged and reliable as they get knocked about and become covered in water and dirt. You also need ones that will take about 200 yards of your chosen line or braid. Mentioning line, it must be said that I remain a bit of a piking dinosaur so I continue to prefer monofilament mainly because of its cheapness, low visibility and the fact that it is readily available. You can get away with using 12 lb breaking strain line in snag-free water but I prefer 15 or even 18 lb. When using braid, and I must admit it does have easy to knot, long life and good bite indication qualities, I tend to use 30 to 50 lb breaking strain. Incidentally, when drifter float fishing, trotting or free roving livebaits floating braid is required, whereas as far as monofilament is concerned if using such tactics it will have to be greased to make it float.

After the rod, reel and line/braid another key aspect of tackle, not least as far as pike safety is concerned, is the need for proper bite indication so as to avoid the deep-hooking of pike. Perhaps the most pleasing way of detecting a bite or run is by using surface floats. They come in a variety of shapes and sizes though all tend to be large and brightly coloured. Slider floats come in slim and more cigar shaped sizes and are useful for dead and livebaits particularly at close range, while the more dumpy, pear or bung-shaped slider is the preferred option for bigger livebaits. Then there are pencil floats which can be self-cocking and are primarily used for deadbaits. More rounded, spherical floats are suitable for dead and livebaiting as well as for trolling, while the dart-like floats incorporating a flight are ideal for long range fishing in choppy conditions, and drifter floats have a vane and are sail-like meaning that baits can be carried to extreme distances subject to a favourable wind speed and direction. Finally, mention must also be made of the sunken floats that are used when, as the name suggests, sunken paternostering using dead or livebaits.

Apart from using a surface float for bite indication the main way of detecting bites is by using an electronic bite alarm. As with all tackle, they come in various models and sizes, and are used in conjunction with two rod rests, the alarm itself being placed on the rear or, more usually the front, rod rest. They can be used as a back-up to using surface floats but are more usually used for ledgering or sunken paternostering, together with drop-back indicators attached to the other rod rest.

We now come to the terminal tackle, namely hooks and traces. Pike fishing usually involves the use of treble hooks and they can be barbed or semi-barbed and generally

Strong, specialist tackle, not least rods and reels, as well as good bite indication are required for catching pike.

two in the sizes 4 to 8 are used depending on the size of bait. The distance they are set apart depends on bait size but as a rough guide 3 to 4 inches suffices for most purposes. They are attached to a wire trace of 20 to 30 lb and about 18 inches long, with a swivel attached to the other end, followed by the leads/ledger weight. If paternostering or popping up baits, a further up-trace of about 12 inches is attached, this preventing bite-offs when pike strike from the bottom thereby increasing the chances of cutting through the line. Sometimes specialist deadbait rigs are used consisting of a single hook instead of a second treble; they are useful when the pike are gulping down the baits because the single hook makes unhooking that bit easier. Finally, I often use a single treble when using a trotted, free roving/roaming or paternostered (float or sunken) livebait. The latter is lip-hooked, this meaning it retains its action much longer, and although some jacks may be lost the larger fish will readily be caught.

The final 'bits and pieces' of tackle required relate to the important business of landing and unhooking your capture. Most obviously perhaps is the need for a large landing net, say of 42 inches, so that it can easily hold a large pike. Next an unhooking mat is required though you could make do if there was a soft unhooking area of, for example, grass close by. A weigh sling is then needed to weigh your catch. Finally, there are the tools to actually unhook the pike and at the very least forceps, together with wire cutters, are needed. The latter are useful for cutting up traces that are badly tangled in the net and could damage a struggling pike.

Some of the various methods and techniques, including rigs, used in pike fishing have already been referred to, but I now want to concentrate in a little more detail on such issues.

Methods and Techniques

Perhaps rather obviously, when baitfishing from the bank, dead and livebaiting are the two methods used, but within these methods there are a variety of techniques.

As indicated, deadbaiting is now the most widely used method of catching pike. This should come as no real surprise as pike are active scavengers on the look out for any dead fish to eat. There are two main aspects to consider, namely static and mobile deadbaiting.

Static deadbaiting usually involves the basic running ledger and float ledger rigs, though float and sunken float paternostering, as well as simple float fished deadbaits are also used. For ledgering and float ledgering, the bottom treble is inserted halfway down the side of the body, with the second treble going into the tail root. This is also the case for larger baits which can be cut in half if necessary. Such rigs are great for clear bottomed waters if you position the bait in an area where pike are likely to patrol such as along the bottom of a drop-off. Paternostering is perhaps the most complex technique as it involves tethering the bait above the water bottom by using a boom attached to a lead/ledger weight and a surface or subsurface (sunken) float. The bait is also mounted as for ledgering but on a shorter trace to help ensure it does not tangle with the rest of the rig. Such rigs are then positioned near where pike are likely to lay up, for instance near weed and reedbeds, overhanging trees and bushes, sunken trees or snags in general. They are also useful if the bottom is weedy as the bait will still be able to be seen by hungry pike. Mention must also be made of popped-up deadbaits which are a variant of the running ledger rig in that, for instance, foam is inserted inside the deadbait or some other buoyant material is attached thereby making it float off the bottom. This again comes into its own if the bottom is weedy or consists of soft mud which could hide the bait.

Static deadbaiting focuses on the pike's highly developed senses of sight and smell, but mobile deadbaiting also targets the pike's sensitivity to vibrations caused by the movement of the bait. First, there is wobbling or, as some prefer to call it sinking and drawing, which is in effect spinning with a dead fish which is hooked head-up on the trace and then cast and retrieved in an enticing manner. A tough and durable dead-bait is needed, one that can stand up to repeated casting, so fish like perch, mackerel and trout tend to be used, though that should not put you off trying softer baits from

PIKE

Keen Yorkshire piker, Peter Hague, enjoys static deadbaiting; he caught this 19 lb 4 oz beauty from the River Aire on a mackerel tail.

time to time. In addition, even half baits and eel sections can also be used. Second, drifter float deadbaiting utilises the drifter float with a vane which is attached to a ledger weight/lead and then the wire trace. The baits are hooked as for ledgered deadbaits and providing the wind is behind you, it pushes the vane and hence the rig and bait enabling great expanses of water to be covered. This is especially useful for exploring likely looking pike-holding areas further afield rather than just concentrating on your own swim. Importantly, and as stated, unless you are using floating braid, the line needs to be greased to prevent it from sinking. This latter comment also applies to those rare occasions when I simply float fish a dead or half-deadbait; again, depending on the current and wind, a larger area of water can be covered.

Turning to livebaiting, as pike are hunters and predators it is no surprise that this leads to many pike being caught. And it is certainly a thrilling way to catch them. For example, what can beat watching the float as it bobs and trembles as the livey does its work. Then all of a sudden there will be a more forceful bob before the float 'plops' and disappears into the depths. A quick wind down followed by a forceful strike and you could be into a large mama that simply oozes power. But alas…let us stop the daydreaming and look in more detail at the techniques involved.

59

First, and at its simplest, it involves suspending a livebait below a float so that it is allowed to swim around. It is commonly referred to as free roving/roaming or, on a river, trotting. It is a very exciting way to catch pike as it allows a lot of water to be covered so increasing the chances of the bait coming to the attention of a pike. The bait is hooked by inserting the bottom treble in the root of the pectoral fin beneath the bait's gills, while the second treble is then inserted at the root of the dorsal fin on the bait's back. Again I also like lip-hooking with a single treble this ensuring the bait retains its action for longer. As with drifter float deadbaiting or float fished deadbaits, unless floating braid is used the line must be greased to stop it sinking. Second, ledgering livebaits, either by the running ledger rig or float ledgering, can be a highly successful way of catching pike. Essentially they are the same rigs for ledgering and float ledgering deadbaits, with the hooks inserted, and rigs, used in much the same way. Third, there is paternostering, both float and sunken, and again they are essentially the same rigs used for deadbaits and used the same way. A difference though is that instead of using two trebles, I again like to lip-hook the livebait with a single treble for the reasons given earlier. Finally, we have drifter float livebaiting which is similar to drifter float deadbaiting although the bait is hooked as for free roving/roaming or trotting. Previous comments about floating braid and greasing line also need to be noted.

This 10 lb summer-caught pike grabbed Steve Rogowski's float paternostered live gudgeon on the River Derwent and produced a spectacular fight.

In passing it has to be pointed out that although both dead and livebaiting are very successful methods for catching pike, many seem to think that deadbaiting always leads to bigger fish while livebaiting leads to more, if smaller, fish. This perhaps explains the fact that deadbaiting has overtaken livebaiting in terms of popularity. However, and for the purposes of this piece, I recently completed a cursory analysis of my captures of 20 plus lb pike. The result was interesting and revealed that deadbaits have indeed caught more 20 plus lb pike than lives; in fact 64 per cent of my twenties came to deads. But this by no means indicates that lives will not also get you the bigger fish because, as the reader will have already worked out, 36 per cent of my twenties fell to lives. Of course, there is nothing scientific, nor is there likely to be anything statistically significant in all this, but it may provide food for thought. Be all this as it may, as this discussion of dead and livebaits now brings me to a discussion of these baits themselves.

Bait

We all know that pike have a vigorous appetite, so when it comes to eating fish, dead or alive, it is not surprising that many and varied fish species prove to be excellent pike catchers.

The majority of pike deadbaits nowadays tend to be sea baits, not least because coarse baits are banned on many waters such as those in the Lake District. In addition, when compared to catching lives, sea deadbaits are easier to obtain being readily available from supermarkets or tackle shops, and unlike coarse deads they also re-freeze very well and can be used for more than one session. Some weird and wonderful varieties have been tried over the years, kippers and gurnards being ones that spring to mind. The latest craze seems to be using blueys, a relative of the garfish, but I have yet to use them. Even so, everyone seems to come back to several old favourites and these are the ones I deal with here, though in no particular order.

The cheap, plentiful and humble sprat accounts for some big pike every year, and my third ever pike, of 29 lb 4 oz, fell to this small, silvery and smelly fish. A drawback, as with sardines, is that they have soft flesh so are probably best used for margin fishing, unless they are used half-frozen or tied on to the trebles with cotton. Sardines themselves are an oily fish so it is no wonder pike are readily attracted. Mackerel are the most popular sea deadbait, one factor being that they are tough skinned and can withstand long range casting. They are used whole or in halves as they range in size from the smaller joeys of about 5 inches to fish of over 10 inches. Herring smell strongly and are a very light colour so can easily be seen in mud or weed. They can also be used whole or in halves. Then we have the cucumber smell of the light, slender smelt which are one of the top baits, being aerodynamic for casting. Finally we have lamprey which is eel-like and full of blood which makes a great attractant. They are durable and cast very well.

The use of coarse deadbaits tend to be dominated by such as roach, bream, rudd and dace. These silver fish of about 4 to 6 inches long make excellent baits, after all

Dead roach and perch are two excellent coarse deadbaits.

they are the natural prey of pike. Perch are another very good bait and believe me the spines do not put the pike off. Eels, in sections or whole are very tough skinned and can be cast to the horizon without fear of them flying off the hooks. The same eel piece can also catch you several pike. Trout, brown and rainbow, are also tough and successful baits suitable for long distance casting, while the silvery pollan is a recent addition to the deadbait armoury not least because they are buoyant, thus being especially useful when you need to fish off the bottom. Having mentioned the most commonly used coarse deadbaits it has to be said that all the others will produce on their day. Examples include ruffe (again do not be put off by the spines), chub, bleak and gudgeon. In fact, gudgeon are perhaps my favourite bait either live or dead. Live gudgeon, usually caught on my favourite Yorkshire rivers have caught me many a large pike to over the twenty pounds mark. They are strong and lively, being able to retain their action for a long time.

Having had a look at baitfishing from the bank, I now briefly turn to using these methods from a boat.

Baitfishing from a Boat

Personally I remain committed to baitfishing from the bank (possibly, as people continually tell me, because I cannot swim!) but pike fishing with such baits from a boat has many advantages. The most obvious one is that you can cover water that cannot be accessed from the bank. The large lakes, lochs and loughs self-evidently come into this category but so do smaller waters such as the Norfolk Broads and even some rivers. The use of a boat enables you to tackle otherwise difficult to reach or snaggy swims as well as allowing you to move quickly and efficiently between swims. Importantly, the thing to get right at the start is the boat itself along with the boat equipment.

Boats and Boat Equipment

Boats range from small rowing boats and even dinghies to high-powered speedboats with luxurious cabins and sleeping accommodation. Such rowing boats and dinghies may be fine for small lakes and stillwaters but for the larger waters a motorised boat is

Lough Ree; Steve Rogowski is bank fishing but often larger waters are better tackled by boat.

needed and they come in various basic hull designs: displacement, semi-planing and planing. In simple terms, these types of hull are suitable for small, medium and large expanses of water respectively. As a rule of thumb bigger boats are safer should the weather deteriorate but bearing this in mind a boat of about 14 ft is ideal for pike fishing, and once the boat itself has been sorted you then need the appropriate equipment to go with it.

First and foremost a means of flotation in the event of an accident is required and so life jackets should be worn at all times; on large waters, especially the weather can deteriorate very quickly. Second, a fish finder/echo sounder helps in locating shoals of prey fish and individual large fish, but they also indicate bottom contours, rocks and other potentially dangerous features and are a general safety aid. Some finders also have an integrated global positioning system (GPS) and these are an added bonus. Third, a suitable engine with a size that matches the boat is required. Other modes of propulsion, such as oars, might be sufficient for a small boat on a small water but in any case are also a useful back-up. Fourth, you need suitable anchors which in turn depend on the bottom terrain of the water. And finally you need items such as boat rod rests, specialist trolling rests, boat seats and a drogue. The latter is a parachute-like device which slows the boat down on a drift, this enabling the angler to cast and cover a lot of water in the process.

Tackle

Much of the tackle used for bank fishing is the same for boat fishing but there are some important differences. When it comes to rods, for example, for many years pikers simply used their usual bank rods on those odd days when they were afloat. This was adequate and produced fish but nowadays shorter specialist boat rods tend to be used, one reason being that such shorter rods are far more manageable within what can be the cramped confines of a boat. Typically these rods are 10 ft long with a 3 to 3.5 lb test curve with a shorter handle because usually you do not need to cast as far when afloat. Other differences in tackle will hopefully become clear in what follows on methods and techniques.

Methods and Techniques

As with bank fishing the two methods that concern us here are dead and livebaiting, both of which include various techniques many of which are drawn from bank fishing. So, unless stated otherwise, the comments above in relation to bank fishing with dead and livebaits apply here.

With deadbaiting, probably the most common technique is simply float fishing a deadbait. This is because ledgering and sunken paternostering are difficult to do from a boat as good bite detection is almost impossible because of the movement of the boat. Any float can be used as long as it can be easily seen though in rougher weather and choppy water conditions the use of dart-like floats comes into its own. And although sunken paternostering has its drawbacks, the surface float version is certainly viable particularly if you want to fish close to a feature. On the other hand, if the intention is to cover water over a wider area then drifter float set up is required and this can certainly be equally productive. A wobbled deadbait is also not a bad idea for covering a wider area.

A more specialised boat technique for deadbaits is trolling which refers to slowly dragging baits behind a moving boat. It really is a very good method of covering a lot of water and catching lots of pike. In warmer conditions pike will come up a long way to snaffle the bait though in cold conditions the bait needs to be kept near the bottom. A good tip, therefore, is to constantly alter the depths at which the bait is set until feeding pike are located. Float trolling involves a sliding float, ledger weight/lead and wire trace with the deadbait attached; the bottom treble is inserted in the side of the bait near the vent and the second is lip-hooked. A variation is bottom bouncing which refers to bouncing a bait along the bottom as it is dragged along. At its simplest a half-moon lead is placed above the trace and, of course the float is dispensed with. Alternatively a variation of the sunken paternoster rig could be used. In both instances there is generally a need for tough baits simply because of all the bouncing about that takes place.

When it comes to livebaits, simply trotting or free roving/roaming with a float can again be an exciting way to cover lots of water. What is more the beauty of doing this from a boat is that the bait can be gently lowered into the water rather than cast, this meaning that it lasts that much longer. A drifted livebait has the same advantages as trotting and free roving/roaming but in addition it allows the bait to travel to greater distances. Float paternostering is also viable, but less so the sunken version or ledgering for the reasons given above in relation to deadbaits.

Trolling is equally suitable for livebaits though it is very important to hook them as indicated for deadbaits earlier, because if it was done otherwise the bait could be drowned by being trolled backwards. Float trolling is the favoured technique as bottom bouncing can soon lead to the demise of the bait.

Finally, mention ought to be made of drift fishing whereby the drogue is used to slow down the drift of the boat while the angler casts and covers a lot of water. As we will see, it is particularly effective as far as lure fishing is concerned, but equally dead and livebait fishing can benefit from this particularly as far as wobbling is concerned.

Lure Fishing

The final main method of fishing for pike is lure fishing and as suggested earlier, when I refer to lure fishing I also include fly-fishing; it may be stating the obvious but after all artificial flies are lures. It is also worth noting 'lure fishing' is a generic term which has largely superceded such as 'spinning' and 'plugging' which usually refer to using spinners and artificial fish respectively. Such ways of catching pike have been around for a long time but, apart from these changes in terminology, there have been some other significant developments over the last forty years or so. For instance, in the 1960s livebaiting and then deadbaiting were the favoured methods as lure fishing took a back seat and was seen as a mainly small fish method. In addition, the lures that were around were small and limited to such as crankbaits, spoons and spinners. All this was to change over the following decades.

Steve Rogowski is not a committed lure fisher but when he does, he tends to use basic lures like these: e.g. spinners, crankbaits, spoons and surface lures.

In the 1970s and especially during the 1980s the importation of lures began to take off and there was a resultant growth in the choice of lures as well as an increase in their size. Instead of 3 to 4 inch lures, larger 6 to 7 inch lures became available. In the 1990s this trend continued with the arrival of 8 to 10 inch or even larger jerkbaits, followed by all manner of large lures, some with half wood and half soft plastic bodies and soft plastic tails. In fact, nowadays soft plastic lures are just about the most popular lures around. But as we will see, that is not to say you will not catch on the many other types of lures that are now available. They come in all shapes, sizes and colours including jigs, spinnerbaits and surface lures as well as those already mentioned. Then we have the flies used in fly-fishing for pike, a technique that has recently become more popular. In short, lure fishing has grown to the point that there has never been as many lure anglers around as there are now.

Tackle

As well as developments in relation to lures, tackle also changed over the period in question. For example, instead of having to make do with a 10 ft spinning rod to meet all your needs, a variety of rods now cater for all the lure types from light spinners to heavy crankbaits and jerkbaits. Apart from rods, the rest of the tackle has also come on a lot.

Echoing earlier comments, although rods are now available for every conceivable lure and lure fishing situation, my view is that sometimes they are designed by tackle manufacturers simply in order to make more money from lure fishers. Having mentioned such a caveat, it has to be acknowledged that a whippy spinning rod is not suitable for such as jerkbaits which require a stiffer action to impart 'life' to the jerkbait. Bearing all this in mind I reckon you can get away with using two types of lure rods, plus one for fly-fishing. For most lure fishing then, using lures such as small to medium spinners, crankbaits and spoons, a rod of about 9 ft and being able to cast lures in the 20 to 60g range will suffice. For jerkbaiting, however, a shorter, stiffer rod is necessary so one of about 6 ft 6 in and being able to cast jerkbaits in the 40 to 120g range will certainly do the business. And for fly-fishing a rod of about 9 ft and rated AFTM (Association of Fishing Tackle Manufacturers) 9 to 11 are fine for pike.

The choice of reel for lure fishing comes down to fixed spool reels or multipliers. As a general rule fixed spool reels are best for lighter lure fishing, say up to about the 60g mark. For heavier lure fishing, especially jerkbaiting, a multiplier reel comes into its own. Some are put off multipliers because they seem complicated to use with over runs and resulting bird's nest tangles being common. If truth be known though, they are easy to use and are very accurate and effective when it come to casting and working lures. Finally, as for fly reels, they need to be light, strong and able to take both backing and fly line as well as a mono leader.

As with dead and livebaiting, when it comes to line for lure fishing the choice is monofilament or braid. I do not know if it is habit rather than anything else (or as I said earlier the dinosaur instinct within me), but I still favour mono especially for lighter work, a breaking strain of 10 lb being about right. However, it has to be said that braid does score over mono in terms of low stretch which means every touch on the lure can be felt. In addition, braid of about 50 lb is certainly best for jerkbaiting as mono is generally not as good in terms of being able to deal with big jerkbaits.

Line for fly-fishing is about 30 yards in length and can be floating, slow sinking or fast sinking. Floating line, unsurprisingly, floats on the surface and is the one most commonly used, being especially useful for shallow water or margin fishing. Slow sinking line is useful in windy conditions as it will not be affected by cross-winds which can drag the fly out of position and spoil presentation. Fast sinking lines are used by boat anglers fishing in deep water or in shallower areas where it is necessary to get the line down fast. The choice for backing line is generally unimportant as it will not actually be used in the casting or landing of fish so mono or braid can be used. Finally, as for the mono leader, this allows better presentation and allows cutting back when replacing damaged traces. A breaking strain of about 30 lb is about right.

Traces for lure fishing including fly-fishing are usually made of multi-strand

67

stainless steel wire with a swivel and clip at each end. Alternatively, a solid trace made from stiff single strand stainless wire can be used, these being particularly useful for jerkbaiting. In both cases the need for good quality components has to be emphasised, and the trace itself should be about 10 inches long.

Before turning to the lures themselves, a brief comment about the rest of the tackle needs to be made. Much of this is the same as that needed for bank and boat fishing – unhooking and landing equipment, for example – but there are differences such as the need for specialist lure bags and landing nets. The former are needed to ensure the lures do not become tangled up together and there are many such bags together with purpose designed, plastic boxes on the market. As for nets, they tend to be round or oval as the traditional triangular landing net used for bank fishing can be cumbersome for the roving approach of lure fishing. Finally, if lure fishing from the bank, it is also useful to have a pair of waders.

Lures

All the main types of lures have already been mentioned – crankbaits, jerkbaits, jigs, soft plastics, spinners and spinnerbaits, spoons and surface lures – but here I want to consider each type in a little more detail, along with flies.

Crankbaits are probably the most common lure simply because they are the easiest to use. Whether you choose the floating or sinking versions of deep or shallow divers, all you do is cast out and then reel or crank it back in and the lure will wriggle its way back. It is the lip or diving vane at the front that makes them work with the more pronounced and horizontal in relation to the body the lip is, meaning the further it will dive. Although they are very easy to use, the speed of retrieve can be important. Put simply, retrieving a sinking crankbait quickly means it will reach its maximum depth equally quickly. Varying the retrieve then means you cover different layers of water, this enabling you to find where the pike are. Similarly when trolling crankbaits, the faster the troll the deeper they will run. As for floating crankbaits, they are particularly useful for fishing over snags: they can be cranked down to just above them and if the lure touches the snag, simply stop reeling and it will float up and away. Of course, in deep water, deep diving and sinking crankbaits come into their own.

Jerkbaits are usually bigger, heavier and, in terms of colours, often flashier than other lures. They are usually made of dense wood and internally weighted, so requiring the specialist rods mentioned above. Unlike crankbaits they depend on the angler imparting action by pulling and twitching the rod, and they come in shallow running, sub-surface and sinking versions. More recently there has been the introduction of hybrid versions featuring soft plastic tails which can be retrieved simply by reeling in slowly which leads to the tail wriggling in a very tempting manner. Slow sinking jerkbaits often need to be slowly teased back giving the pike plenty of time to strike, this being particularly useful in winter when the pike's metabolism slows down. Conversely a shallow running jerkbait can be retrieved speedily in the warmer months

'Spinning' Steve
Appleby with a superb
19 lb 8 oz pike caught
on a crankbait from the
River Derwent.

when the pike are after anything that moves. Having said this sinking jerkbaits are generally more versatile as they can be fished at various depths by simply counting down to the chosen depth and then retrieved until the pike are found. The speed of retrieve can also be varied. Once the pike are found, it is hard to beat the sight of pike following and then aggressively seizing a jerkbait.

Jigs are a relatively new lure in the British piker's armoury, consisting of a rubbery body impaled on a hook with an integral moulded head usually made from lead. They can be bounced along the bottom or worked in a vertical fashion from a boat, and they can certainly produce the goods in terms of catching pike.

Although they have been around for many years, soft plastics were initially considered as small fish lure though this was to change in the 1990s, not least with the introduction of the Bulldawg with its blunt nose and rubbery tail. It was the wriggling tail that seemed to attract the pike and make this so successful a lure. Thereafter a weird and wonderful range of soft plastic lures appeared followed by realistic fish-looking and feeling lures known variously as shads, swimbaits and replicants. Indeed, one of my piking partners, 'Spinning' Steve Appleby, has certainly taken a liking to these lures, so much so that after having spent years using crankbaits and spoons, soft plastics are now a firm favourite. I recall taking him to the Ouse and after a few hours of him failing to catch told him to try a shad; sure enough he did and went on to have seventeen pike haul for over 100lb. A little like crankbaits, soft plastics are usually best fished by simply casting and retrieving them, and again, this time like jerkbaits, they can be counted down and slowly retrieved until you find where the pike are. You will also often find that they are taken on the drop as you are counting. Apart from a slow, straight retrieve which can be particularly effective in colder weather, a more erratic one, by jerking and jigging the rod, will induce takes especially in warmer weather.

Spinning blades on lures have been around for many years and though perhaps not the most popular of lures, spinners and spinnerbaits, the latter having blades away from the body of the lure, do catch many pike. They are usually more successful in shallower water with good visibility, especially spinners, while if anything spinnerbaits are better in deeper, cloudier conditions. Spinners are best fished by casting them out and retrieving them as soon as they hit the water, this enabling the blade to rotate immediately. They can also be fished just beneath the surface so that the rotating blade creates a wake, such a technique being useful for tempting pike hiding in submerged weed. As for spinnerbaits it is the fact that they vibrate so much that makes them particularly effective in coloured water. What is more they are easy to use as all that is needed is a simple cast and retrieve.

One of the oldest types of lure is the spoon which actually is derived from the common tablespoon. They were usually silver or copper coloured, and the way they weave and wobble in the water can prove irresistible to pike. Nowadays you can get them in various shapes, sizes and colours and they surely deserve a place in every lure fisher's tackle bag. Although perhaps underrated and less popular than they were it must be remembered that in the past they were very successful on such as Norfolk Broads and on the loughs of Ireland. Larger spoons are suitable for large trout reservoirs and natural lakes, while the smaller ones are best for shallower waters like rivers, canals and pits. Incidentally, one of my favourites, Tobies, come into both categories. All are easy to use as a simple cast and jerky retrieve is often all that is needed.

Surface lures float on the surface, their action being imparted by the angler. There are various types and it is exhilarating to see a pike engulfing one of these lures. For example, poppers and chuggers have blunt faces which maximise water resistance and cause them to bubble and spit in response from rod jerks, while prop-baits have propeller-like spinners at their head and tail which rotate and churn up spray thereby attracting pike. Or again crawlers flip-flop across the surface usually via a double-lobed lip. Finally, there are soft plastic creature-like lures such as a frog or mouse look-alikes; although they sink they are designed to be hopped or skipped over and between such as lily pads and weeds. All such lures are usually more effective in the warmer months when pike are hungry and spend a lot of time in shallows or near the surface.

'Spinning' Steve Appleby working his fly on a reservoir.

Finally, there are the flies for fly-fishing for pike to briefly consider. They are typically in the 4 to 6 inch range, though you can get larger ones, and they vary from natural colours to more bold even gaudy ones. Rabbit skin and buck tail are two of the traditional materials used to make them but such materials are now complemented by artificial fibres. They can also be weighted for bouncing along the bottom and even have small spinners attached. It goes without saying that, as with other lures referred to, it is a good idea to have a varied selection in your tackle box. After casting simply slowly retrieve and wait for that electrifying strike when a hungry pike snaffles the fly.

Bank and Boat Fishing with Lures

Bank fishing with lures, including flies, probably remains most popular despite the growth of boat fishing. After all boat fishing is not allowed on many waters and even when it is, many canals, drains and small pits or rivers do not really justify fishing from a boat.

A stealthy approach is needed for bank fishing so as not to disturb any pike lying in the margins. Thereafter, all that is required is to cover the water thoroughly with a

71

series of fan casts. If there is no action, change the colour of the lure, its size or the lure itself. It goes without saying that the above comments in relation to the various lure types need to be borne in mind. Larger waters can prove to be more difficult simply because the pike might be further out and beyond casting distance. Targeting features like adjoining streams or weed and reed beds is a good idea, but it also pays to find out what is underneath the water too. This can be done by such as asking local people or by the tried and trusted way of plumbing the depths. Alternatively such large waters may be best tackled from a boat.

When it comes to boat fishing with lures many of the comments made earlier in relation to boat fishing with baits apply, for instance, the need for a suitable boat, safety equipment and so on. Then, once the boat has been launched and you are out on the water you can either fish statically or adopt a more mobile means. If it is the static approach that is favoured, simply anchor up near a chosen feature and you are ready to go. Alternatively the mobile approach involves both trolling and drifting, both of which allow a lot more water to be covered. Importantly remember that flies can also be trolled and drifted as well as, of course, being used statically. Again, whether you are fishing statically or you are mobile, it can be important to vary the lures used both in terms of type, size and colours. On occasions the pike will be very selective about what they will strike at, so continually experiment until success is found.

Conclusion

I now want to conclude this chapter by stressing, perhaps a little belatedly, the need to land and unhook pike safely. Despite their appearance and reputation, pike are delicate creatures and need to be treated with care and respect. This is especially so in the warmer months when, as I hinted at, they can almost give their all in the fight after being hooked. Initially then, you must have the landing and unhooking tackle referred to earlier and after this there are various steps that need to be followed.

First, it is important to strike quickly following a run or take so as to prevent deep hooking. Second, unless you are experienced and can land a pike by 'chinning', the pike should be netted and placed on an unhooking mat or, as I said earlier, as a last resort, soft grass. Third, the pike should be lifted slightly by sliding one hand under the gill flap while the other uses the forceps to do the unhooking. You could also straddle the pike if you are afraid it might start flapping about and if the hooks are too far back the forceps can be put through the open gill arches to unhook them. Fourth, the pike should be placed in the weigh sling for weighing or being carried back to the water after a quick photo if so required. Fifth, the pike should be returned to the water and rested until it is ready to swim away. Incidentally, on occasions a pike might need to be retained for a while, so that a photo can be taken when the rain has stopped lashing down for example. In such circumstances the pike can be retained for as short a time as possible, either in the landing net or better still a pike sack/tube. If all of these steps are followed carefully, the pike will be fine and none the worse for being

Steve Rogowski 'chins' a 26 lb plus Broadland pike before carefully returning her.

caught. Furthermore, a small but significant step will have been taken to ensure they are around for future generations of pike anglers.

So there you have it: an overview of pike and pike fishing in the British Isles. In a chapter such as this I can only provide an outline of this fascinating fish and ways of catching it. But remember, pike and pike waters need to be continually looked after and conserved; although progress has been made in this regard over the last fifty years we must continue to be watchful and on our guard. There are and will be various challenges to the sport over coming decades, this being something I return to in the final chapter of this book. In the meantime, I hope that everyone who reads this chapter will be enthused and encouraged to get out on the bank or boat and enjoy the thrills of catching this supreme freshwater predator fish.

3
Catfish
Simon Clarke

The catfish, that is the Wels, Danube or European catfish, or *Silurus glanis*, is simply the biggest and hardest fighting predatory freshwater fish in the British Isles and across Europe, not least France and Spain where many British anglers travel. Arguably catfish offer anglers the ultimate angling test. Being a mysterious, ancient fish, and one of nature's winning designs, they are unpredictable and can be a real challenge to catch. But when hooked, pound for pound they fight harder than any other fish I have caught and, furthermore, every catfish capture is a real achievement. By the way, to say that they are predators is not strictly true as they are omnivorous and have a wide range of diet. Having said that, they are certainly predator in the sense that fish as well as crustaceans make up a significant percentage of their diet, this in turn meaning that unquestionably they can be caught using predatory fishing methods.

Although there are some unsubstantiated earlier records, they were almost certainly brought into England from Romania in the 1860s by the Acclimatisation Society. The most successful introduction was by the Duke of Bedford to lakes on the Woburn Abbey Estate in the 1880s. Since then they spread slowly until the 1980s after which their distribution increased, now being found in over four hundred waters mainly in England but with a few in Wales. The species is not found in Ireland, and although they were introduced to Strathclyde Loch, Scotland in the early 1990s there have been no recent verified captures. All this means, however, that a majority of anglers in England and Wales now have a catfish fishery within forty miles, this making them a viable target for many anglers.

Despite being large fish, with big fearsome-looking mouths, catfish are docile on the bank and easy to handle, so there is definitely no reason to be afraid of them. My view, and admittedly this comes from a long time catfisher, is that anyone having the chance to fish for them should jump at the opportunity. As I have heard said by so many catfish anglers, 'if you catch one catfish, you're hooked!' This in turn reminds me of my first encounter with a catfish at the Airman Pit, Bedfordshire over twenty years ago.

I had just moved to the area and after spotting the water I went to visit, seeing a number of anglers fishing with bite alarms which was not too common a sight in those days. After polite enquiries I was told they were carp fishing but they also mentioned that catfish were in the water. I had always been interested in unusual fish and from the

Simon Clarke with a 62 lb catfish; pound for pound they are very hard fighters, this fish taking twenty minutes to land even with decent tackle.

moment I heard about the catfish I just had to catch one. I did not really know how to go about it and there was only limited published information at the time; a chapter in Frank Guttfield's *The Big Fish Scene* and one in John Golder's *Top Ten* book. Nevertheless, I had a couple of sessions that summer using dead freelined rudd but without any success. My luck started to turn the following winter with the Catfish Conservation Group being formed and my contacting Bob Baldock. He was very helpful and even came over to the lake during the close season to walk round and give me some advice.

I prepared for the new season and duly arrived on the water at around 10 pm to get a swim for the midnight season start on 16 June. However, I was shocked to find every swim on the lake already occupied except for one tiny spot on a steep bank in one corner. Nevertheless, I quickly set up there, with trout pellet and liquidised liver paste on one rod and squid on the other. I had mentally prepared myself for a long wait and was not really surprised there was no action during the night and through the morning. In fact, the Airman Pit was an old clay quarry with clear water and a reputation for only producing catfish at night. The long June day dragged on and I had brought one rod in as my friend Keith Lambert arrived at around 6 pm to see how I was getting on. 'Nothing doing' I said with him asking why I only had one rod out. 'I was really waiting for later and wanted to re-bait ready for the night' was my reply. 'Get that rod cast in, you've got a chance at any time' he ordered and I duly re-baited the rod in question with the paste and cast back in. We sat back for a chat and no more than five minutes later the rod I had just cast was away with the alarm screaming. I scrambled down the bank and struck into a hard-fighting fish that hugged the bottom. 'Could it be a cat?' I excitedly thought to myself. Keith was the first to spot the fish properly as he was at the top of the bank and had a much better view. 'Take it easy it's a catfish' he urged as I coaxed the fish into the landing net and then triumphantly onto the bank. Stunned, yet exhilarated, I weighed my first catfish at exactly 9 lb. I recall that I did not get another run during daylight at the lake for the remainder of the season but in truth it really did not matter; I certainly was hooked on catfish for life.

In this chapter I aim to provide an overview of catfish and catfishing in the British Isles. First, I deal with the fish itself focusing on such as its biology, habitat and behaviour, followed by size. I also look at 'other' catfish species; that is, catfish that are not the Wels variety but nonetheless are species you could come across. Second, and more substantially, I turn to catfishing itself and in so doing deal with catfish waters, when to go, baits, pre-baiting and loose feeding, tackle, rigs and methods, and hooking, playing and landing a large catfish. In concluding, in essence I sing the praises of my favourite fish in the hope of encouraging the lawful spread of catfish, this large and hard-fighting freshwater predator.

The Catfish

Silurus glanis is the largest fish of the widespread *siluridae* catfish group which are found across Europe and Asia. It is native to eastern Europe and Asia, occurring as far west as Germany and as far south as Iran but has been introduced to many other countries including France, Spain, Italy, Sweden, Turkey, the Netherlands and, of course, the British Isles.

Biology, Habitat and Behaviour

The catfish can be identified by the elongated, scale-less body which has a strong upper body and a laterally flattened tail. They have a very small dorsal fin with a small spine and four to five dorsal soft rays, one anal spine and 90 to 94 anal soft rays, and a caudal fin with 17 rays. They have paired pectoral fins with one spine and 14 to 17 soft rays each. Their paired pelvic fins are positioned behind the dorsal fin with one spine and 11 or 12 soft rays each. They can also easily be distinguished by their six barbules, two long ones either side of the mouth and four shorter ones under the lower jaw. Sex can be determined in two primary ways: first, the flap of skin behind the vent in males is thin and comes to a point, whereas females have a thicker and shorter flap of skin; and second, mature (7 lb plus) males typically have a thicker and rougher pectoral fin with a rough leading ray, this becoming more pronounced in later spring as fish become ready to spawn.

Catfish vary greatly in colour this in turn being dictated by the environment they live in. Typically, in clear water the fish are very dark on the top and the flanks with a very white belly, whereas in coloured, muddy water they are normally very pale. They can also change colour quickly with, for example, fish moved from a pale environment to a dark one changing colour within an hour.

In British Isles waters, as stated in effect in England and Wales, catfish mostly reside in lakes and in common with other fish species. As an alien species, they may only be stocked into enclosed waters though they adapt to a wide variety of water conditions. They are very hardy and generally solitary, preferring quiet water, usually with a soft bottom such as mud. They love cover, and will lay up for long periods under overhanging trees and bushes, in weed beds, and any other dark places such as under snags and in deep water. They are most active at night, though in coloured water in particular they are also active in the day.

When it comes to reproduction, males pursue females just under the water surface often before a thunderstorm on warm and stifling days. This behaviour is an indication that spawning will occur the same evening or the next day. The male nudges the

Richard Garner and Simon Clarke with two lovely French catfish.

77

The male pectoral fin: the leading ray is thick and rough.

female in the anal region, swims under her and may lift her so that her back is above water. He then wraps himself around the female for 10 to 12 seconds, before they separate and she sinks slowly to the bottom and discharges eggs, with the male following to release milt. This process can be repeated several times over one-and-a-half to two hours and the water around the nest is milky from sexual products. The adhesive yellow eggs are laid in depressions formed by the male pressing down with its body in mud or in weed beds, in shallow 40 to 60 cm water. Approximately 400,000 eggs, with diameters around 2 to 3 mm, are then guarded by the male during the day and night, with his tail fin moving every 3 to 5 minutes to ensure adequate oxygen supplies. They hatch after 3 to 5 days with the juveniles soon eating fish fry and invertebrates before graduating to larger foodstuffs.

As suggested earlier, catfish are omnivorous, primarily predating and scavenging and therefore feeding on a wide variety of natural food like worms, snails, crustaceans, aquatic insects, and small fish. At adult sizes they will also prey on crayfish, fish, frogs, rats, waterfowl. They use the incredible suction created by suddenly opening their large mouths to take in prey. In addition, both the top and bottom jaws have pads of inward sloping, soft teeth used to grab and hold prey. They then use their two pairs of crushing plates to soften the food before swallowing.

This 35 lb 8 oz pale fish was part of Simon Clarke's best ever catfish haul; six for over 190 lb from Elphicks Fishery, Kent.

Simon Clarke and Graham Lawrence with a solid 115 lb River Ebro system Spanish fish.

The business end of a large catfish showing the grabbing teeth at the front of the mouth.

Size

How large catfish grow has been the subject of much rumour and debate, both as far as the British Isles is concerned and abroad. As for the ultimate size for the species, there has been talk of fish over 400 lb and up to 600 lb, usually said to be 'from Russia'. Personally though, in years of interest in the species, I have never seen a photograph of one over 240 lb and I strongly believe it is unlikely a catfish can exceed 350 lb. Their ultimate size will no doubt be endlessly debated but what we can say, from close monitoring of their development, is that they grow quickly in length up to approximately 6 ft. They then start putting weight on and generally 'bulking up' while their length growth slows, the maximum recorded length being around 8 ft 9 in. As for weight, even at 300 lb, they are one of the largest freshwater fish in the world, and one with the most numerous to grow to over 100 lb .

Catfish have been present in the British Isles for over 120 years and to date have not grown anywhere near as large as those in the southerly areas of their natural range. Indeed, growth rates here are significantly lower than abroad with 3 to 4 lb per year an average and no fishery has ever had a consistent growth rate in excess of 7 lb a year. The slower growth rates are mainly due to climate and food availability, with the British Isles being at the northern end of their range. The exact potential and ultimate size is difficult to estimate as many catfish have been imported at a variety of weights and determining what is, for example, an 'English grown' fish is not easy. Having said that, since their introduction to Woburn Abbey it has been reported, albeit without photographic evidence, that the Shoulder of Mutton Lake was drained over forty years ago and fish to over 70 lb were removed. Apart from that instance, until the 1980s there are no reports of catfish any larger than the 43 lb 8 oz fish caught in 1970 from Tring Reservoirs, Hertfordshire. Since the 1980s and particularly in the 1990s, with more catfish being imported many large catfish have been caught to 130 lb. However, the largest 'truly grown' fish I know of is around 70 lb and the largest imported catfish to be 'grown' here is around 91 lb, being less than 10 lb when it arrived. There are now at least three waters containing catfish over 100 lb but all of these fish were imported at that weight.

There are now many waters across southern Britain containing big catfish with more than fifty fisheries containing fish in excess of 50lb. But due to the number of huge imported fish the British Record Fish Committee has suspended the record, so it remains officially at 62 lb, being caught by Richard Garner from Withy Pool, Bedfordshire.

Other Catfish Species

It is important to point out that in the British Isles you may encounter catfish that are not the Wels variety. These other catfish species, also present in some European countries, are uncommon and generally much smaller. Identification is mainly an issue if the fish are small but in any case there are three species to note.

First, there is the Channel catfish, *Ictalarus punctatus*, a native of North America with a wide range from Canada right down to the southern USA. Channels normally inhabit rivers and can grow to around 60 lb, but rarely exceed 20 lb. It has a small under-slung mouth and eight whiskers, four on the bottom jaw, and two at the side and two coming out from the top jaw. They generally tend to be slate grey in colour though when small, say under 8 inches, they often have spots on the flank which gradually fade as they grow larger. There have been many thousands of such catfish imported over the last twenty years and sold through the pond and aquarium trade. Inevitably, over the years many of these have thrived and grown too large for their owners, being released into waterways as a result. This is illegal and should not be condoned but seems to have shown that these catfish are not an invasive species. I know of no authenticated cases of them breeding, and while many survive, grow and have subsequently been caught to low double figures, in general they do not appear to thrive. Finally, and unusually amongst catfish species, the Channel catfish is common in albino form, and a large percentage of the imported fish have been like this. Indeed, if you hear of an albino catfish being caught it is 99.9 per cent certain it will be a Channel.

Second, in mainland Europe there is one rare catfish which is very closely related to the Wels catfish, even though you are unlikely to ever encounter it. This is Aristotle's catfish, *Silurus aristotelis*, which is only found in and around the Akelhoos river system on mainland Greece. It is very similar in looks to a Wels, but can be identified by the fact is has only four barbules, with just two under the lower jaw.

81

Third, there is the Bullhead catfish, *Amieurus melas*, which is another customer from North America though thankfully it is very rare in the British Isles. In fact, I have not heard of any being caught in the last ten years. In the past, like the Channel catfish, they had been widely imported for the ornamental fish trade, but in the last twenty years there have been very few in circulation and I have not seen one for a long time. They are small, growing to about 2 lb though usually only to about 1 lb, and they are shorter and more squat than the Channel, also usually having a darker colour, often with a brown tinge. The mouth is also on the front of the fish as opposed to being under-slung or over-slung. In common with the Channel catfish it has eight barbules, four on the bottom jaw, two at the side and two on top.

Finally, we come to what might be called 'other catfish which are not catfish'. I am referring to the occasions when inexperienced anglers will report having caught 'catfish' but in some cases they are actually referring to the bullhead/millers thumb, *Cottus gobio*, or stone loach, *Barbatula barbatula*. Both look like a miniature catfish, but as neither grow to more than about 6 inches long, confusion is limited.

Catfishing

I now turn to fishing for catfish, or put another way, as the title of this section states, catfishing. As mentioned earlier, there are now over four hundred waters in the British Isles containing catfish, the majority being in the southern half of England but there are some in the north of England and some in Wales. By far the bulk of these waters are stillwaters. Although there are some rivers that contain catfish, probably as a result of flooding, generally fishing for them there is not a viable proposition. Among the stillwaters though, there are a number of commercial fisheries with excellent facilities especially for those willing to travel and fish a long session.

Finding a Catfish Water

Stated simply, far and away the best source for information on catfish fisheries is the Catfish Conservation Group (CCG). If you want full fishery information on location of waters, control, facilities, stock and cost then look no further than the CCG book *Guide to UK Catfish Waters*. Such guide books are notoriously hard to keep up to date but this publication really does help narrow down your potential waters. However, bear in mind new waters are being stocked with catfish each season, so it is also worth keeping an eye on such as the angling press and the internet as well as asking at your local tackle shop.

The CCG list of waters also contains details of rivers known to produce catfish though, as I said, targeting fish in rivers is not really recommended as no river has a viable population to target. Very occasionally fish do get caught, but there are probably far more rumours and myths than actual fish. If you do want to try rivers then find out as much information as you can and I would strongly advise you to invest time in

pre-baiting (see below) to maximise your chances of attracting
fish to where you are fishing.

When to Go

Once you have selected where you
want to fish, in my view it is
important to consider when to
actually go catfishing. Biologically
speaking catfish are fish of pretty
basic design and their metabolism
is significantly affected by water
temperature; put simply, the higher
the temperature the faster the
digestion rate and the more active
they are. On the other hand, in
cold weather they have an ability
to completely switch off and so
avoid loss of condition.

So when is the time to fish for
them? In general the answer is as
soon as the water temperature hits
9.5°C the catfish will be feeding.
This is normally around mid-
March depending on the area of
the country. Shallow southern

The Catfish Conservation Group's Guide to UK
Catfish Waters *is invaluable in deciding where to catfish.*

lakes seem to be the first to start producing and even in the cool weather of the spring
there is some good catfishing to be had with multiple captures even more common
than in the summer months, as I well found when fishing one spring.

When I first started catfishing every lake containing catfish had a full close season
between 15 March and 15 June. Though I supported the close season in principle,
three months is a long wait especially as often during these months the weather could
be lovely and I would yearn to fish. Today the close season for lakes only operates on
very few fisheries, and most of those close only for a shorter period. For catfish anglers
this has proved a huge boost to their prospects, especially as catfish are inactive for the
majority of time during the winter months so it is pretty much hit and miss targeting
them at that time.

My first attempt at early season fishing was some years ago. The previous season a
couple of mates had had some catfish in late March from Yateley Match Lake,
Hampshire and I decided to try my local lake the next spring. March proved cold that
particular year, but it became slightly milder in the first week of April so I went to the

lake for a single night session. I measured the water temperature at a cool 10°C and set up. There were just two other anglers on the lake, both carp fishing, and I laughed to myself at the silly prospect of catfishing in conditions more suited to pike angling. As darkness fell I was well wrapped up for the night and snuggled down more in hope than expectation. Yet to my surprise less than 30 minutes into dark one of the baits was taken, but dropped before I could strike. As the lake contained quite a few pike perhaps it was one of those? Another 15 minutes went by and a tug on the bait kept me alert. A further five minutes and a slow jerking pike type run kept going and I struck into a fish with a reasonable fight following and eventually landing the fish without actually knowing what it was. I peered into the net and blow me it was a catfish of about 10 lb. Significantly it was in good condition and relatively fat with no sign of poor condition as you might expect from a fish lying up for winter. I put it straight back, re-bait and re-cast. Over the next hour I had a couple more pulls on both baits but no takes. After that the action stopped and nothing happened until I was woken up by a run just as it was getting light. I quickly grabbed the rod, which hooped over and I was into a heavy fish which ran hard to the right; 'surely this could only be another cat?' I thought. And sure enough it was as 5 minutes later I netted a lovely fish which tipped the scales at just over 25 lb. 'What a great session!' I mumbled to myself, but to cap it all after re-casting I had another take 15 minutes later and landed another catfish of around 10 lb.

Simon Clarke with a spring-caught catfish. He has had more multiple catches in spring than any other time; this was one of a three fish haul.

Bob Warren with a lovely early season 35 lb catfish caught on luncheon meat, a good bait in cool water conditions.

To summarise, I had caught three catfish in a session for only the second time in ten years of catfishing and subsequent spring sessions have produced more multiple catfish catches than during warmer months. Perhaps this is because cats feed less often in cooler water but often when they do feed, many fish feed at the same time.

As with all fishing, relative temperature change is also important, so a quick rise from 6° to 9°C may trigger an early feeding spell. In such cool water conditions stick with soft baits such as luncheon meat and lobworms. Livebaits can also work well when fished close to the bottom. Do not be surprised if you get finicky takes as the appetite of the catfish in cool water is less than in warmer spells. You may also find, and as already suggested, that pike are attracted to your baits in cool water conditions, so be prepared to adjust your tackle accordingly if this is the case. As water warms up during April and into May, changing to livebaits will usually prove successful. As the water temperature increases further position livebaits closer to the surface as the catfish will be feeding more actively and aggressively. Always watch out for any sign of fish striking to locate feeding areas. Meat baits and other soft baits will still work throughout the summer, though problems from nuisance fish are likely to increase. Throughout the summer until the end of September is peak catfishing time so make the most of it.

As the weather changes during October with the autumnal nights getting cooler, the catch rates start to slow but there is still some great catfishing to be had. At this time of year the fish are at their heaviest and this is when many big fish are caught. I believe that the fish may sense the cooling conditions and this triggers a feeding period as fish prepare for winter.

The catfish feeding rates will drop dramatically after the first heavy frosts, with catch rates dropping accordingly. Commercial fisheries with high fish densities where anglers' bait makes up the largest percentage of catfishes' diet typically fish on for another month but by December pretty much all catfishing has ground to a halt. There will be short feeding spells in the winter but they are so infrequent that it makes fishing for them pretty much a rather thankless, difficult task. It is still worth watching the weather though as often there are mild spells in December or January, during which time a few catfish get caught, usually I suspect by baits landing right on their noses.

Although catfish do feed during the day and night typically the best fishing is to be found at night. This is because there is a reduction in bankside activity after dark and also the catfish's natural scavenge and ambush tactics are usually more suited to the dark hours. In clear water lakes night fishing is certainly usually the best, but in coloured water lakes you are more likely to catch a catfish anytime of the day or night.

The importance of watercraft in all of the above cannot be overstated. Admittedly the advent of so many heavily stocked commercial fisheries has meant watercraft is often neglected, but it remains a key success factor. And by watercraft, I refer to, for example, reading a water to judge where you think fish will be, where they will patrol, selection of swim, methods and baits, positioning yourself and choosing where to cast your baits. When all this has been taken into account, it is then about continuing to read the water by watching for signs of fish whether it be bubbles, swirls, fry scattering and so on and thereafter modifying your catfishing accordingly.

Baits

I now come more specifically to baits, though many have been mentioned in the previous section. Although catfish have a broad diet and you have a chance of catching one using virtually any bait, it is no surprise that certain baits prove more successful than others. Furthermore, the selection of bait will often dictate the rigs and methods used.

Beginning with natural baits, worms are probably the best bait for catfish. You can freeline, ledger or use a pop-up rig with them, and although they have the downside of being eaten by most other fish, using large bunches at night will minimise the hassle. You can also fish a pop-up rig to get the worms off the bottom which can be particularly effective for catfish while also meaning they get less attention from other species. Pop-up rigs also offer the advantage that the worms are less likely to bury themselves in the lake bottom while their wriggling also attracts catfish. Lobworms are usually the best worms to use though dendrobenas are worth a try especially as they are very active.

Leeches are a good catfish bait with the one main advantage being that it is the one bait that you can be 99.9 per cent sure that when you get a take it will be a catfish as they do not seem to attract takes from other species. They can also sometimes trigger a lot of takes, though admittedly they seem to be more effective on some waters than others. The medicinal leech is the usual species that is used, both here and on the continent. They have a unique snake-like swimming action which you can observe when they are in water. I am convinced that this swimming action is what proves such a good draw to catfish. Remember though that you have to be very careful about presentation of leeches to minimise them tangling the rig and/or levering themselves off.

Deadbaits are ideal for catfishing, with freshwater deadbaits normally the most effective especially roach, rudd or eel section. As catfish have such a sensitive sense of smell it is no surprise that a fresh dead fish is highly attractive to them, and furthermore they will be able to detect it from a considerable distance. I always prefer to catch a fish and kill it to use it fresh if possible, though some blast-frozen species, for example eel and lamprey, available through your local tackle shop will also catch. Sea deadbaits can also work, particularly if pre-baited and used on heavily fished waters. In order of preference, I use sprats, sardines and mackerel. Any deadbait can also be used in sections.

Squid and shellfish are also effective and are key baits in the catfish anglers' armoury with squid being able to be fished in a number of ways. The calamari squid is usually about 6 to 8 inches long and can be used whole, with the head removed or even in small pieces. Freeline or popped-up squid have both worked well for me.

Not for the squeamish: dead roach, whole or halves, make good catfish baits.

Incidentally, squid is probably my third favourite catfish bait after worms and livebaits. When it comes to shellfish baits, although they catch catfish, they often attract carp and so they may be difficult to use. Bait presentation can also be difficult and fiddly with such baits as they are soft, while they are also susceptible to being nibbled off over a period of time by smaller fish. Even so, cockles, sea mussels and whelks have all caught catfish and may be well worth a try, particularly on well fished waters.

All such deadbaits can be put directly on the hook or you can use a short hair if you prefer. With directly hooked baits, try to just lightly hook the baits in a firm area, so that you can cast them but also can pull the hook out on a strike. For directly hooked baits I would also recommend using bait shields, which help reduce the risk of the hook turning and hooking back into the bait when striking.

I now come to livebaits, and must say I have caught more catfish on livebaits than any other bait, though admittedly I do fish them more than static baits. I think that partly it is down to confidence and I really am very confident using livebaits. Although catfish are scavengers looking for easy food, it will come as no surprise that they predate on live fish. The most common coarse fish like roach, rudd and perch are all ideal baits and can usually be easily caught or scooped with a large landing net after dark. If available, small tench, carp or crucians are also good bait species. On some waters and at some times certain bait fish species tend to work best, but to my mind it is far more critical to position your bait in the right area than worry too much about the species you are using. Whatever you use, baits of 2 oz to 10 oz are best. As catfish have very large mouths in relation to their body even modest fish can snaffle a large livebait. If you get stuck with only very small baits can you use two or even three on the hook. Whatever are used they can be fished in open water or near fish holding areas such as overhanging trees or weed/reed beds.

Moving to liver, it is underrated as a bait but well worth using. It is soft, bloody, cheap to buy and easy to use, often proving to pick up some of the biggest fish. You can use pretty much any type of liver, whether it is chicken, lamb, pig or ox. All of these readily leach blood into the water over a period of hours and have accounted for many catfish. Kidneys and hearts are also baits to consider; both also contain lots of blood which is gradually released into the water and can prove a great attractant, particularly on hard fished waters where such a different bait may well score.

Meat baits, such as luncheon meat, have proved very consistent catfish bait and, as I said earlier, they have been particularly effective in the cooler water conditions of spring and autumn. I think that their soft, easily digested nature makes them particularly palatable for catfish when their digestion rates are slower in these colder conditions. Incidentally, as luncheon meat is also attractive to other species, a tip is to use large baits; do not hesitate to consider even cutting a small tin of luncheon meat into three as it will still normally do the job. Other varieties of tinned cooked meats and those from the chilled food cabinet at the supermarket are worth a try. All can be fished on the hook, but are normally better fished on a hair.

Pastes offer the ability to combine ingredients and flavours, yet still offer catfish a soft palatable bait, something which they prefer to harder baits. With paste it is easy to alter bait size and flavour, of course.

Catfish generally do not really like boilies as they are hard, with relatively little smell. The fact that so many catfish get caught on boilies is largely due to the sheer number of boilies thrown in and the number of hookbaits cast out. For every catfish bait cast out on an average fishery there are probably fifty carp baits, so even if a catfish takes one in thirty carp baits and regularly takes catfish baits, the catch rate will seem higher on boilies. Carp boilies are usually made from good quality ingredients and flavours, so despite the hard texture and limited flavour released, they do offer the catfish a food source, hence they do get taken. If boilies are fished over a bed of pellets or other free offerings the attraction becomes even greater to catfish and they will sometimes come and hoover up. If you do want to use boilies stick to natural flavours and use bigger boilies or multiple baits to target bigger catfish and avoid small carp. Some new 'boilie-pellets' are now available, which are softer than traditional boilies and are usually cylindrical in shape. The softer texture and faster breakdown of boilie-pellets are more palatable for catfish and have more effective scent release so are likely to be more effective.

Fish pellets which are formulated to attract fish, will catch catfish with the oily nature of halibut pellets seeming to score best, particularly in warmer conditions when the catfish's digestion rate is at its peak. As with boilies, larger baits will often prevent nuisance fish from taking your bait. Halibut pellets are available up to 28 mm, or multiple 20 mm pellets can be fished to form a large hook bait. Hair rigging is essential as pellets cannot be hooked and large baits would impede hook penetration. Pre-drilled halibut pellets are available making putting them on a hair easier than trying to drill them.

Pre-baiting and Loose Feeding

Pre-baiting and loose feeding can certainly help to improve your catch rate. Pre-baiting helps attract fish to areas you bait up and get them used to a type of bait. I have fished some lakes where it is very difficult to access the good swims and in these

Pre-baiting can lead to big catfish, such as this mint conditioned fish for Kevin Midmore.

circumstances I have successfully used pre-baiting to get fish feeding in other areas. On catfish waters with low fish densities pre-baiting can also really help. I suggest using squid or liver to do this, with the option of also using chopped fish. My tip is to build up pre-baiting over a period of weeks and then to actually try fishing. If it has not worked first time, my advice is do not give up but try again.

Loose feeding is the term used for when you are actually fishing and throw in loose feed to attract catfish or to get them feeding. If you have pre-baited or are fishing an area where you think or know fish reside then a few free offerings loose fed will ensure your hook bait has a good chance of being taken. On the other hand, if I am fishing a water which has not been pre-baited, say a heavily fished commercial water, then you can loose feed to attract fish to your swim. In this circumstance I tend to use smaller bait such as maggots/pellets and chopped up hook bait samples. Several species of fish will often respond and hopefully the catfish will sense the activity and also come in to feed.

Tackle

I now come to the tackle for catching catfish, and it may be stating the obvious but stout, robust gear is definitely recommended for these hard-fighting fish. Heavy carp or pike gear will certainly do the job, but better still is to obtain some well designed, specialist catfish equipment. In particular, the rod should have a through action to absorb the powerful runs and cope with big fish. Actually a specialist catfish rod tends to be shorter than most carp and pike rods, with a slightly larger test curve; say, 9 to 10 ft 6 in and a 4 even or 5 lb test curve.

Sturdy baitrunner style reels are the order of the day for catfishing with a tough main line such as *Big Game*, *Pro-Gold* or other trusty monofilament brands. My advice is to steer clear of low diameter carp mono lines which are not up to the rough, tough job of catfishing. Braids can also be used if you prefer. Importantly, test the clutch on your reel before you fish to make sure it is as smooth as possible. Before coming to the terminal tackle, do not forget all the other essential equipment like landing net, unhooking mat, unhooking tools such as forceps and pliers, and weigh sling.

Now for the terminal tackle, which is the only part of your tackle which normally comes into contact with fish and is therefore the most critical. Catfish will test every bit of it to the limit, so good condition, top quality terminal tackle is a must, to avoid missed takes or lost fish. This is especially so if you are fishing for really big fish and in snaggy waters; you certainly must up-rate your tackle to match the conditions.

More catfish are lost from inadequate hooklinks than any other cause, either through breakage or wearing through. A quality *catfish* hooklink is a vital element of your catfish tackle; there is a big difference between a catfish hooklink and a carp hooklink that someone says 'you can use that for catfish', or 'that will do for catfish'. I have heard enough tales of lost fish and taken enough snapped off carp rigs out of catfish to know what I am talking about. *Catfish-Pro 'Catlink'* is an ideal braided hooklink suitable for all methods except livebaiting. The aramid fibres are hard wearing and have great abrasion resistance. There are some other brands on the market but always ensure they are up to the job before using them.

If you are livebaiting, monofilament hooklinks are generally best as their stiffer nature reduces tangles. You can use heavier reel lines, such as 20 lb *Big Game* or 22 lb *Pro-Gold*, or low memory monofilaments such as *ESP Stiffy* or *Catfish-Pro Toughlink*. Pike can be a problem when catfishing and in such situations *Catlink* will usually land most pike, but if you need to be sure switch to true cut-proof hooklinks such as *Pikesafe*, a soft, knottable PVC coated wire or *Kevsteel* X, a kevlar/wire hybrid braid which is limp in nature and minimises the risk of catfish spooking.

A proper catfish hook is a vital part of your tackle not least because a very strong one is essential. Bear in mind that many catfish are often lost when inadequate hooks straighten during a fight. Catfish hooks offer key advantages such as a wide gape, a long shank and an offset point for accommodating bulky baits while also aiding hook penetration on the strike, and a thick gauge wire to avoid hooks opening out. To my mind the *Maruto Eagle Wave* is the best on the market. But whatever catfish hook you use always check to ensure they are sharp before use; much of the catfish's mouth is bony, consequently holds can be light so a sharp hook really is essential.

Having sorted out your catfish hook, you really must make sure you use one big enough for the job. Even a 10 lb catfish has a mouth 4 to 5 inches wide which means a small hook can get 'lost' with there being a good chance of striking it straight out of the fish's mouth. Also remember to always match the hook size to your bait; for

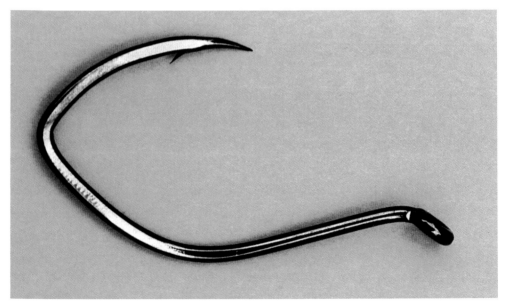

The Eagle Wave *hook is the most popular catfishing hook; its distinctive design makes it ideal for bulky baits.*

instance, a big lump of luncheon meat needs a 1/0 or a 2/0, or for livebaits use ones between a 2 and 2/0 depending on bait size. Circle hooks are also proving quite popular for livebaiting as they have a good hook up rate and they are well worth a look to see if they work for you.

In passing, if you are fishing for catfish 'carp-style' with smaller baits such as pellets or boilies, you may want to move to a shorter shank hook for rig balance. This is fair enough but just ensure it is man enough to handle a catfish.

When it comes to other key items of terminal tackle, you must use strong swivels of at least 80 lb, in conjunction with good-sized rubber beads to act as shock absorbers and 3 to 5 oz leads/ledger weights. To ensure your hook point is not masked and that livebaits stay on the hook, using bait shields is recommended especially when using barbless hooks. These dense rubber discs are hooked after the bait and they grip the hook to keep the bait in position. Finally, buoyant balls of foam or polystyrene from ¼ inch to 2 inches diameter are ideal for popping baits up and making up special catfish rigs, while livebait rigs can be enhanced using rig rattles these being clipped on to attract catfish as well as keeping the bait more active. Mention of rigs brings me specifically to these, along with methods and techniques.

Methods, Techniques and Rigs

By far the most popular method of catfishing in the British Isles is by using static bait methods and techniques; that is fishing from one swim to a chosen feature and in effect waiting for the catfish to come to you.

Freelining is the simplest method for catfishing when using static baits, the latter including all baits except livebaits. It is generally underused even though it is ideal for margin fishing for two primary reasons. First, the fish does not feel resistance when it picks up the bait, giving more confident takes and less dropped baits. Second, the limp line on a freeline minimises the chance that the catfish will sense or touch your line and spook off and leave the bait. If you want to freeline but need to cast a reasonable distance, you can either use a heavier bait or use a disposable weight, such as a pebble in a PVA bag. Keep any bobbins light and easy to drop off. Swinger type indicators are not suitable for freelining, or indeed ledgering static baits, unless you are fishing bolt rigs, though these are not necessary for catfishing. Remember that when scavenging and picking up static baits, catfish are often nervous and cautious consequently being sensitive to resistance. This means, of course, that if your set up is not set right you will experience dropped takes.

If you need to fish at range or accurately to a feature, ledgering is the method of choice. In such a case use a good-sized lead of 2 to 4 oz and a low resistance run ring on the lead link to minimise the risk of the 'lead bumping'. Another important factor to bear in mind when ledgering is to avoid tight lines; catfish do not like lots of lines in the water, so slackening your line to allow it to lie on the bottom will increase your chance of a take.

I now turn to the rigs, beginning with the end rigs for non-livebaits. Thus, for boilies, pellets, deadbaits and meat baits you can fish baits on a running ledger set up with the bait on a hair. Importantly, a big enough hook must be used, one which should also be matched to the bait size. For softer baits it is also worth using bait shields on the end of the hair before the stop to bear the weight of the bait and reduce the risk of it coming off on the cast. Worms, pastes, liver and other soft baits can also be effectively fished straight on the hook. Squid can be fished on a hook or hair rigged. Importantly, popping baits up when you have weedy or sour bottomed lakes can help.

When it comes to livebaits, a ledgered livebait is the best all round technique for catfishing, as it has accounted for more catfish than any other. There are many variations to ledgering, all having their specific purpose. The key decision is to determine where you want to position your bait in the water and to choose your rig to suit that need. Essentially it amounts to positioning a bait anywhere between the lake bed and the surface. This is because depending on the water, conditions, temperature as well as other factors, you will be more successful at certain levels in the water. In simple terms, in the coolest conditions catfish will be sluggish and close to the bottom and will pick up baits there, whereas in the warmest conditions they will love sub-surface baits. It is for the angler to judge and experiment to find what works where and when you are fishing.

Running ledger rigs are the primary method to which you can attach an end rig with varying amounts of buoyancy to position your bait. In cool weather a straight ledger with no buoyancy will position a bait on, or close to, the bottom. Attach a polystyrene ball or foam ball on a hair to lift the bait up in the water. The amount of buoyancy will either gently lift or suspend the bait at the level you want to fish.

This brings me to the poly-ball rig, a running ledger rig with a poly-ball or foam ball attached. Over many years it has been, and still is, an extremely effective rig. The size of the ball is adjusted to match the size of the bait. Normally it should be buoyant enough to lift the bait when at rest. The bait then keeps trying to swim away from the ball with the result being that it is more active than on a normal ledger rig. The ball itself is normally fished on a 6 to 9 inch hair attached to the eye of the hook, though if you are using soft foam balls you can push them on to some soft silicon and push that into the hooklink to form an inline poly-ball rig. If the bottom is weedy or sour then use a slightly larger poly-ball to prevent the livebait from being able to swim down into the weed.

Once you have set up your rig and cast out, I recommend you do not use a bobbin or swinger; rather just tighten up and set the baitrunner mechanism on your reel to 'on'. The takes on livebaits tend to be pretty aggressive with the catfish usually steaming off at high speed, with the only exception being normally in cool water conditions when takes can be jerky and half hearted.

There are variations to the poly-ball rig. With the standard rig, the area that the bait works is limited by the length of the trace you fish. If you increase the amount of line you pay out then the fish will be able to work a wider area. You can also fish the rig with a long hair; simply set the hair length at the depth you want to fish, affix a larger poly-ball and cast out. The poly-ball then stays on the surface, effectively allowing you to float fish your bait. You can monitor the poly-ball on the surface to ensure your bait is working well and if it stops for a long period you know your bait may be in weed or even have died, so you can check it by giving it a gentle tug. This surface poly-ball can also give you early indication if catfish are around because the bait will panic and the poly-ball will bob around more violently.

The inline poly-ball rig is ideal for river conditions and as an anti-tangle version of the normal rig. The key thing to remember is that the catfish will often take the whole rig when it strikes, so use soft foam poppers that can squash if taken so as to minimise the chance of a missed take or the bait being rejected before you can strike.

Another buoyant rig is the dumb-bell rig which is a real favourite of mine and works really well when you want to fish livebaits close to the surface. In fact, I have had the majority of my best catfish on this rig in recent years. It is a surface rig that enables you to fish your bait in the top 10 inches of water, and critically it keeps the area under the bait clear so allowing catfish to strike unimpeded. The anti-tangle nature of the rig also enables you to fish it with braided hooklink making bait fish movement more natural. Simply fish the dumb-bell on a running ledger and the buoyancy will automatically bring it to the surface. I usually lip-hook the bait or hook it in back just behind the dorsal so that it swims away from the rig. Takes can be spectacular; as they are so close to the surface you often hear the take before the alarm sounds as the catfish strikes and makes a swirl. As with all livebait rigs I fish the dumb-bell set up with the line straight off a baitrunner without a bobbin. It is suitable for water depths of up to about 10 ft deep.

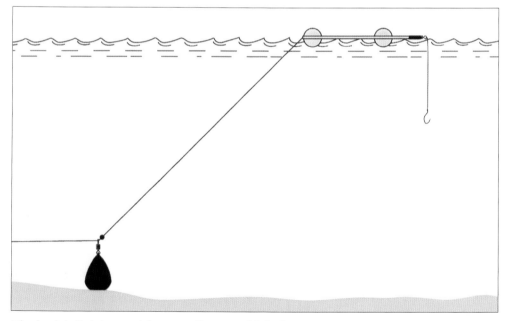

The dumb-bell rig is one of the most effective catfish livebait rigs.

All smiles for this huge catfish caught by Graham Lawrence on a 5 inch trolled plug.

An adapted, submerged version of the dumb-bell rig has also proved very effective when fishing leeches or worms. The rig is fished on a running ledger as with a livebait dumb-bell, but it is not as big and has smaller poppers on. It is best to simply cast out, keep your line tight to the rig, set it on the rest and then let out a measured amount of line equivalent to how much you want to pop the rig up. As you let out line the rig will lift up. The particular advantage of doing this for leeches and worms is to prevent them burying in the bottom because, as with the livebait dumb-bell, the area under the bait is clear. I recommend fishing these rigs between 1 ft off the bottom up to mid-water, although many people have had success allowing the bait up to just under or even on the surface.

Paternoster rigs are most suitable for deeper water, over 10 ft, when you are looking to fish in the upper layers. One version, the 'cat-o-copter' rig, is a paternoster rig with an additional poly-ball under the hook link which serves two functions: first, to lift or slide the hook link and the bait to the desired depth and second, it adds buoyancy to help keep the rig vertical in the water. As with all paternoster rigs the hook link should be kept short, say 6 to 8 inches, using a stiff hook link to minimise tangles. The rod is then set upright in a beachcaster style, with the line under reasonable tension to the rig, without pulling it too far off vertical. The reel can then be set with the baitrunner 'on'. You will usually see the rod top knocking as the bait works, and runs are often very fast and powerful.

Finally, a free roving float fished livebait can be very good if you are able to fish the rig effectively because if you can get the bait roving around it can cover more water than any other livebait method. You can move the bait around to different areas, and the float is a sensitive and immediate indicator for a bait panic or takes. For this to work ideally, you need plenty of room on a fishery and favourable wind conditions to drift a boat out, as repeated casting tends to affect the bait activity.

Obviously, there is an element of using mobile or active methods in free roving livebaits, but generally when I mention mobile or active fishing methods I am referring to lure fishing. Actually it has to be said that there has been very little lure fishing for catfish in the British Isles. It is a more common method in Europe in big lakes and rivers but our often crowded small lakes are seldom empty enough to be lure fished properly and what is more many waters have stringent rules on lure fishing designed around pike fishing. Having said that it could be well worth a try if you have the right water as when it has been used there have been catfish caught. I would try mid or upper water slow fished spinners and jig shads or drachkovitch rigs along the bottom. Trolling with plugs can also bring success.

Hooking, Playing and Landing a Catfish

Bites, runs or takes from catfish will normally be pretty aggressive. Whilst they are often shy and sensitive creatures, when out on the feed and especially when they take the bait things can become fierce and aggressive. This is then what normally happens:

97

To land big catfish, especially from a boat, gloving is the simplest method but check where the hook is first. A firm grip on the bottom jaw is essential.

there is a grab, then a split second delay, followed by a screaming run. You should wind down hard and strike to set the hook, after which the fun really starts.

As I said above, catfish have a lot of bony areas in the mouth, and if you hook a catfish and lose it soon into the fight with a hook pull this is normally because the hook has not penetrated sufficiently and bounces out when the fish turns. But if it is properly hooked you can expect a long hard fight during which the fish will normally stay deep for most of the time. In shallow water you may get a slap of the tail at the beginning. You must stay calm when playing catfish and keep everything smooth and uncomplicated, even if that is sometimes easier said than done. You may experience odd bangs on the rod during the struggle, followed by a moment of slack line almost as if you have lost the fish. This is caused by the catfish's tail whipping round and striking the line; as it comes free you get the moment of slackness.

As the catfish starts to tire it will gradually come up to the surface, but this is the time to take particular care. As the fish gets close I always slightly loosen the clutch to accommodate late dives on a short line. When the fish is really tired it will stay on the surface but this is another time to beware because catfish can swim backwards, this being especially so when the fish is ready to be netted. And when it comes to netting, you must make sure all of the fish is in your landing net before you lift it. If you get really stuck with a big fish you can hand land catfish by grabbing the lower jaw. This requires an element of bravery and a decent glove, and it goes without saying that you need to watch out for where the hook is to make sure you do not end up with a hook in you.

Once the catfish is on the bank, careful handling is essential to prevent additional stress to the fish. Wet the unhooking mat before you lay the fish down gently. As I said at the outset, they are probably the most docile of all fish on the bank so really do not be afraid. The fish may snake or slap about but that is about it. The vast majority of catfish are hooked in the side of the mouth where it is soft, so check where the hook is and remove it. Take care to weigh catfish safely and quickly, and if your sling is not large enough weigh it in the landing net. If you do not have scales large enough, measure the catfish and then it is easy to estimate weight by length. For example, a 4 ft 7 in catfish will be around 40 lb and a 5 ft 2 in one will be about 60 lb and so on up to 6 ft 6 in which is likely to be 100 lb. If you are taking photographs, ensure you hold the fish over the mat and as low to the ground as practical so that if it slips you can lower it back on to the mat to get a better grip.

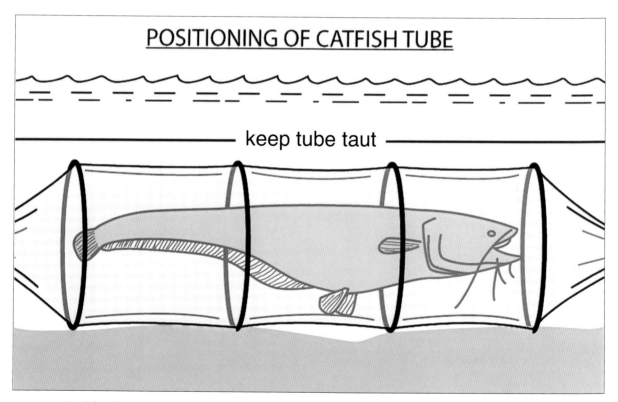

POSITIONING OF CATFISH TUBE

keep tube taut

Catfish tubes are the safest way to retain fish but correct setting up is essential; remember to keep them for the minimum time and to check regularly.

I cannot stress too strongly the need to keep the fish out of the water for the minimum period of time, and be careful to watch out for signs of stress. When stressed, catfish start to change colour by becoming paler so if you see any such colour change return the fish immediately to the water. Then ensure it has fully recovered, if necessary supporting the fish until it is breathing strongly and swims away.

If you need to retain catfish, they should be retained for the minimum period required and only using appropriate methods. You can use a specially designed catfish tube, a type of keep-net that opens at both ends and that can be pegged out. You can also use a stringer, but only if you are experienced or have been shown how to use one. They are the safest way to retain large catfish and involve using a soft nylon cord of about ten metres long. A loop is tied about one metre from one end and the stringer cord is passed into the fish's mouth and out directly behind the gill cover *ahead of the gill rakers*. The cord end is then tied back onto the loop in the cord. The stringer cord passed through the mouth should be kept short with only about 3 inches play on it. Finally, remember that catfish should never be retained in keep-nets or carp sacks as they are unsuitable and dangerous to the fish.

Conclusion

Although a non-native species, catfish are undoubtedly a welcome and invaluable addition to the predatory freshwater fishes of the British Isles. To repeat something I said at the outset, pound for pound they are probably the hardest fighting fish to be encountered by the adventurous predator angler. In this conclusion, as well as singing the fish's praises, I want to encourage the lawful spread of the species as well as describing how the reader can become more involved with this strange, fascinating fish.

Despite being a non-native species, catfish can be stocked into enclosed stillwaters in England and Wales subject to certain requirements, the primary one being that they must not be within a flood plain. If the enclosed stillwater has an outflow, then gravel traps or screens would normally need to be fitted to make doubly sure that there is no risk of escape into river systems where control is much harder. If you are interested in stocking catfish you need to apply and the application will be considered based on the regulations regarding the water concerned and additional submissions from other bodies. Input is sought from English Nature, the Environment Agency (EA) and the Centre for Environment, Fisheries and Aquaculture Science, the scientific arm of the EA. If the water is an enclosed stillwater not in a flood plain then there are not really any major reasons not to get a licence.

It must be remembered that catfish offers fisheries and angling clubs a great opportunity to provide an additional attraction to their water as well as addressing the shortage in catfish fisheries in many areas. Many people who have not experienced catfish are sometimes wary about stocking them but they need not be. The plain fact is that they make an excellent addition to waters as they are not an invasive species and do not have a harmful effect on where they are introduced. Although they have bred in such waters, the success of the breeding is normally poor because the British Isles is at the northern end of their geographical range and young fish grow slowly and are heavily predated on by pike and large catfish. On a positive note, they are predatory scavengers and as such are useful to fisheries in mopping up dead and dying fish, anglers' bait and nuisance species such as signal crayfish which have decimated many fisheries. Indeed, my view is that they are the only fish that have been able to control such crayfish populations so perhaps the EA should even consider using catfish to do precisely this.

Mention needs to be made of the CCG again. More than with any other species perhaps, the growth of catfishing together with general assistance to such anglers can be attributed to this group. Since 1984 it has been the catalyst for the growth of catfishing in England and Wales and has been one of the main single species angling groups. Its aims on formation are still in existence today and include the conservation of existing, and promotion of new, catfish stocks and to recommend correct angling methods, treatment and careful handling of the species. In short, readers of this chapter who want to develop their interest in catfish and catfishing further would be well advised to join the CCG.

Finally, I hope this chapter has been interesting and informative. Remember though, that one of the most fascinating and attractive things about catfishing is that we are still learning a lot about it. Rigs, methods and techniques are changing as we discover more about this fascinating species, all this being something that especially appeals to me. In short, I would certainly urge you all to get out and enjoy the buzz of fishing for the Wels catfish.

4
Eels
Steve Ormrod

This chapter focuses on the European eel, *Anguilla anguilla*, and, of course, fishing for them. For many, perhaps even a majority, a key question is why choose eels as a target freshwater predator species? Such people consider the eel a real nuisance, eating any baits carefully set out for other target species. It is also the twisty, slimy snake that wrecks rigs and covers everything in skin-like mucus. This may help explain why this predatory fish attracts so much dislike and misunderstanding, but this was not always the case and is certainly not the case for those of us who love to target the species.

Going back into history there was a totally different attitude towards eels, though admittedly it was often gastronomic values as opposed to sporting ones that were to the fore. Even so the Egyptians treated the humble eel as a sacred creature whose equal was the gods themselves. The Greeks considered them to be 'king of fish', being a valued delicacy and cure for all kinds of maladies, while the Boeotians thought them worthy of sacrificial offering to the gods. Gastronomic values still ring true today with, for example, Japanese diners eating up many, many tonnes of eels a year. And one must not forget that in parts of the British Isles jellied eels remain very popular.

In trying to answer the 'why choose eels?' question, perhaps my own eeling experience helps. I started fishing for big eels way back in 1974 when regular expeditions to the English Lake District fishing for pike, perch and trout saw accidental captures of eels. One summer's afternoon I went 'a wandering' and followed a small brook from one of the lakes to a small, secluded tarn. The weed was prolific making it difficult to present the worms under the obligatory bobber float. I was wandering along the brook where it entered the tarn, staring hopefully into the deeper holes amongst the streamer weed when I detected the shadowy form of an eel by the near bankside. Lowering the worm in front of it, the eel immediately struck, engulfing it on the spot. A quick strike and I was 'in'. What a great scrap ensued, with it weighing in at just over 3 lb, being a monster compared to the snigs or small, young eels I usually encountered. Fortunately, the hook slipped out while it was in the net making it an even more pleasurable encounter. After that, I read as much as I could about big eel fishing and had a lot of fun camping out and fishing nights in the Lakes. My long-standing personal best eel of 5 lb 12 oz was caught one night during 1976 in the margins of Esthwaite and gave me a real fright. These experiences really turned me on to the bigger fish though it was not until the late 1990s that I resurrected my love and obsession in fishing for big eels. Haunted by dim memories of my days in the Lakes as a sallow youth, from 1997 to 2003 I fished avidly for them in the summer, never getting close to that personal best, but catching a lot of fish to 3 lb and 4 lb plus. After 2003 I felt rather burned out and had a break from the big eel obsession. But as I write, I have undergone a bit of an eel fishing renaissance in my quest for a big English catfish, as most waters I fish for the cats also contain decent eels. There are other reasons why many are fascinated with and thus target eels.

There is their mysterious and intriguing life cycle, the many myths and legends associated with them and, not least, the fact that they are voracious and efficient predators. These then are some of the things I deal with in this chapter. I begin with a discussion of the eel itself and its life cycle, before looking at some eel myths and legends, and what constitutes a specimen eel. I then turn to actually fishing for them beginning with their location and habitat, and the eel fishing calendar. Tackle, tactics, rigs and baits are covered prior to looking at hooking and playing, and handling and photography. Some eel fishing stories are also related during all this before, lastly, I refer to current serious concerns about eel stocks.

Steve Ormrod with an excellent 4 lb 10 oz eel from a Cheshire estate lake.

A decent eel provides a great scrap.

The Eel and Its Life Cycle

The eel is an unmistakable creature with its long, rounded muscular body. It also has a continuous fin that starts at the dorsal and continues along the body, round the tail to the anal vent. Two small pectoral fins serve to balance the body which is covered in a thick protective layer of mucus thus enabling it to move swiftly through the water. Below this are tiny scales, undetectable to the human eye, which are deeply embedded in thick skin. In freshwater, skin pigment varies, this being determined by surroundings and habitat. Colours range from yellow-clay brown, through to chestnut and onto vivid greens and even dark grey or jet black. It is not unusual to catch two-tone eels, for example, half dark grey and half green which indicates the eel has been semi-submersed in silt (grey) and weed (green).

The eel's operculum bone found under the gill cover can be used to age it, a bit like counting tree rings. Using this method, John Sidley once caught a 7 lb eel and decided to have it mounted in a glass case. He removed the operculum and estimated the fish to be 68 years old. He then vowed never to kill an eel again. Whilst this is probably exceptional, it is not uncommon for most 'barren' female eels to live well beyond 20 years.

Eels have an excellent sense of smell to counteract their poor eyesight. It is thought that 98 per cent of the food an eel finds is via its sense of smell. If you look at an eel's head, you will see two small nodules on the tip of the upper jaw and small olfactory portals along the snout too. They, like pike, also have a very good neuromast system of lateral nerve sensors. This enables them to home in on interesting vibrations, for example a wounded fish in distress which then means an easy meal.

The distribution of the eel in the British Isles is widespread, so much so that it is probably easier to list waters where they are not likely to be. Having said that you can find them in rivers, brooks, streams, drains, canals, dykes, reservoirs, estate lakes, gravel pits, park pools and farm ponds and so on. As the following discussion of their life cycle shows, they really do make a long, arduous journey to find a comfortable home.

As with all things *Anguilla*, the eel's life cycle has to differ in that it is catadromous, meaning that it is born in saltwater but develops in freshwater. This is the reverse of the life cycle of the Atlantic salmon, which is anadromous, that is born in freshwater and develops in seawater. Perhaps the best place to begin this intriguing story is when the females get the urge to return to their birthplace to spawn. For instance, a female eel will have spent several years getting fat in her freshwater home, say a decent-sized farm pond. One year she will suddenly get a calling to procreate. So on a dark, drizzly autumnal evening she will start her incredible journey, maybe after taking one last meal. Her body will have changed from the usual brown/green to burnished silver. Her eyes now literally bulge from their sockets on a narrow head built for speed so as to aid her journey. Her metamorphosis started a few weeks earlier and will continue until she reaches the sea. Silently sliding through the wet grass she reaches the local brook and is joined by many others of her kind. They swim with the flow to where it joins the local river. She will not feed, relying on her great fat reserves to sustain her. A few days later they amass in great numbers and head out into esturine waters to join the younger males gathered there. They then embark on a three year journey back to the Sargasso Sea off Bermuda in the Atlantic Ocean. Here, our female mates in depths of 1300 ft, lays her eggs and dies. The new generation are then born as tiny, leaf-shaped larvae called *leptocephali*. In fact, they were originally classed as a separate

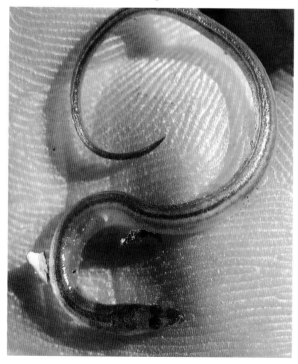

A 'glass' elver – the eel as it enters our rivers.

species before it was realised they were eel larvae. These fragile creatures are then carried by the Gulf Stream to our shores where they adapt and change along the way to become elvers, or glass eels, so called because of their transparent state. Males tend to be much smaller than the females and very rarely move inland, preferring to remain in brackish waters of estuaries and quiet coastlines. It is the females that make their way up our river systems to their freshwater retreats, usually during May/June.

At this stage the young eels are at their most vulnerable and natural predators, including pike, take full advantage of the bounty as do the elver netsmen. Their numbers are vast though, with each being on an unswerving quest which means they will even try to tackle vertical obstructions. As they move further up the rivers they become coloured (yellow eels) to match their new habitat, though the change is more than just skin deep with eyes, internal organs and gills all changing to adapt to fresh-water. They really are amazing creatures as the young 'snigs' disperse up the many connecting brooks and streams.

Eels can travel considerable distances from running water to the inland stillwaters and canals of their choice. Our female will stay in the brook until one dark, damp night she intakes water and oxygen to store in special pouches. She then closes her gills and slithers up the bank and out overland. No-one yet knows how they select their inland residences, but once in their new homes the females go about their lives as the fish we angle for. However, just one more incredible transformation remains. Depending on which food sources are predominant, our female eel adapts her mouthparts, this being another reason early speculation included that there were different species of eels in freshwaters. If her habitat mainly supports invertebrates, crustaceans and insect victims from land and air, she develops a long, narrow snout with tiny teeth ideal for rooting around crevices and silt patches for prey items. These eels probably specialise in feeding on the eggs of fish and amphibians. Opposite to the 'narrows' are the 'broads', predators par excellence. They are primarily fish-eaters, but will also scavenge and take all manner of other prey opportunities that come their way. This eel has a wide, flat mouth with larger needle-like teeth. They have very powerful jaws to crush their victims with the lower jaw slightly protruding so aiding the capture and gripping of prey. You would probably expect such a 'fish-cruncher' as opposed to the 'snail-sucker' to grow to a larger size but you would be wrong, it is quite the opposite. All the huge eels over double figures have tended to be narrows. Why this should be is uncertain, but perhaps there are more concentrated nutrients in an invertebrate diet rather than one mainly of fish.

Our female will now quite happily spend a few years in her freshwater haven, growing from a few ounces to several pounds in weight depending on the venue's food supply and its richness. Most spawning eels are in fact around 1 to 2 lb, though with odd exceptions above this weight. So, the cycle is now almost complete, but what happens next is particularly important as far as the specimen hunter is concerned. Either she will get the urge to return to the sea to spawn and die, or she will ignore the call and spend the rest of her life happily getting bigger, becoming a dominant

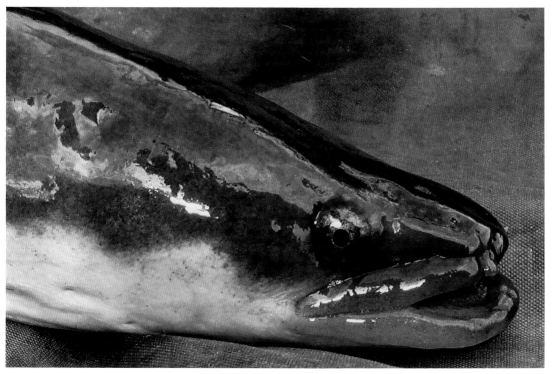

The broad head of a predatory eel.

predator in her home. This is another *Anguilla* enigma because most animals have 'in-built' procreation and fecundity instincts so as to ensure the natural survival of the species. Not always so with the eel, however, and we call these non-maternal fish 'barren' eels, these being the ones we long to catch. You would think they are rare but until recently they have been fairly numerous and they are very efficient predators. So let us look at such specimens in a little more detail, as knowing about their characteristics and behaviour is key in understanding how to tempt and catch them.

A first point to note is that these fish are predominantly nocturnal hunters, with only waters with good depths, permanent shade and underwater cover likely to see any daytime activity. Her home will be in the most inaccessible of places to fish, for instance amongst the snags and underwater cover like sunken tree branches and roots, fallen masonry and discarded flotsam. If deep silt is available she will burrow down in it too with only her head protruding just in case a hapless easy meal strays too close. Eels tend to rest, rather than totally sleep so if you are brave enough to fish close to obvious lairs you will get takes, but they will very quickly leave you snagged up. It is possible to achieve success by 'snag-fishing', but you need to respond very quickly and have very strong tackle indeed. It may not be easy to catch such fish but illustrating just how a big predatory female eel feeds will help.

An overhanging feature involving branches and tree roots can produce large eels.

Damian Wood admires his fine 2 lb 8 oz Staffordshire stillwater eel.

It is high summer so the mere's water temperature is high in the shallows and cooler in the deeper holes. A nice south-westerly breeze has been pushing all manner of deceased insects and invertebrates into the margins. As the sun sets and the breeze dies to a soft ripple, the small rudd go on a feeding spree, gobbling up the free meals. At about the same time our female eel, now a respectable 4 lb plus after a few years of healthy feeding, slides from underneath her fallen tree-trunk lair further along the same bank in a slightly deeper, sheltered area. She tests the water and lingers to see if she can detect anything moving near her home but so far there is nothing.

Her acute sense of smell draws her attention to the shallows further down the bank where all manner of interesting things are lying in the margins. Off she goes, snaking her way along the silty bottom. As she glides effortlessly along she passes a bit of commotion in a nearby gully where bream are feeding gregariously. It does not interest or daunt her as she continues on her mission to track down more curious smells further along the bank. As she nears the area of feeding rudd her neuromast sensory system goes into overdrive; there are lots of prey here this evening. Snaking sinuously in a rapid 'S' pattern movement she gathers momentum as a target is selected. From below she can decipher a vague silhouette that corresponds with the signals she has received. The strike is swift and soon to be fatal. Quickly, she turns around amidst the swirls of a very confused and panicked shoal of rudd to home in on the death-throes of her victim. The poor rudd did not know what hit it as it falls haplessly to the bottom with the tail severed and hanging on by the outer skin. Suddenly, there is a rush of water and darkness as it is engulfed headfirst by our smart female eel.

Wounding and then returning to consume, as sharks do, is just one of the eel's efficient feeding tactics resulting in maximum return for minimal effort. Satiated for now, she turns and heads off on a well-known patrol route along some deeper troughs well out in open water. However, she will not refuse a good nibble at the decaying rabbit corpse she comes across en-route. Taking a good grip on the soft underbelly she spins her flexible torso many times, a bit like an alligator, eventually tearing off a good-sized chunk of flesh and innards. Our eel is a very dextrous scavenger as well as a hunter being able to swim forwards, backwards and side-to-side. What an easy meal this one was.

Suddenly though, she senses danger nearby; perhaps the statuesque shadow of a heron and just in case slides off into the silty deeps. As the sky lightens a few hours later, it triggers her to return to her home to rest up during daylight. But even now she detects an easy meal, this being a large bunch of worms curiously dangling in mid-water. She cannot stop the urge to feed, not least as eels do have huge appetites. Gripping the severed heads of the nearest worms she bites down. A bit more is also engulfed as she turns and moves backwards a little towards her lair. She then detects a strange resistance and releases the prey only to see it swiftly disappear in a rush of bubbles and silt. Rubbing tired eyes and cursing his luck our big eel angler reels in a mangled bunch of lobworms. Our eel has had enough for the night and settles down for the day within her snaggy lair.

Myths and legends

Of all freshwater fishes, none equal the amount of mystique and conjecture concerning the eel. It was not until the 1920s that the eel's incredible life cycle was realised by Johannes Schmidt, a brilliant young Danish marine biologist who tracked the developing eel *leptocephali* in its stages back to the Sargasso Sea. Even now, we still do not fully understand eels and in many ways they remain a mystery.

Early thoughts about the eel's biology were rather far fetched and confused. Some said eels formed from corrupted earth, a certain type of morning dew or even slime impregnated by the sun's rays. Others that horse hairs and the gills of other fishes were the beginning of eels. A more down to earth and understandable theory was the idea that conger eels were simply overgrown freshwater eels, although we now know they are a completely separate species.

Then there was the theory that there were at least four types of freshwater eel – green, brown, silver and those smaller brethren which are as clear as a wine glass. In 1684 an Italian gentleman Francesco Redi observed that adult eels disappeared into the sea and that young eels came out of it. Though he had no idea of what happened in between these strange events, he thought that perhaps the eels procreated just off the shorelines. Others were still way behind in their thinking, and even in 1862 a Mr D Cairncross asserted that the eel's progenitor was a small beetle apparently because they shared various similarities! Then there are the tales of the mass arrival of the glass-like elvers, and the great exodus of the juvenile eels leaving freshwaters under the cloak of night to make their way back to the Sargasso to answer a far-off call of nature. With their eyes morphing ever-bigger and the change of pigmentation to vivid silver perhaps it is no wonder the eel was considered as something rather unworldly.

Tales of monster eels have also emerged over the years though often with scant evidence of their existence. Admittedly on the other side of the globe in New Zealand there resides a freshwater eel of absolute monstrous proportions called *Anguilla dieffenbachia*. It lives in dark water-filled mountainous caves and large baits such as roadkill possum are used to catch them. But the monster eels one hears about from our shores are often far harder to believe. For example, one early evening a professional eel netsman retrieved his fykes expecting a large bounty. The net was proving particularly heavy but he was not really surprised as the eel run that particular springtime had been very good. Surprisingly though, when the first sections of the net came in they were devoid of fish. Then, as he pulled up the last section of the long net over the gunwale of his boat, he gasped in awe. A thick, coiled body of some 8 inches in diameter squirmed in front of him. Then, a huge head with eyes the size of milk bottle tops poked out of the coils. The netsman is said to have sworn that it glared at him with murderous intent. Quickly, he released the knot on his net and let the monster slither away.

Then there is the tale of the 24 lb eel that was caught by the son of a respected lady in the early twentieth century. The story caused much excitement, but it later turned out that her son had been sea fishing and caught a conger. Finally, there is Loch Ness' monster to consider and if one seriously takes some of the claims made, then it could be a gigantic freshwater eel.

But can big eels like the above live in our waters? Perhaps, as just because we do not encounter such beasts regularly does not mean they do not exist. As mentioned, barren eels can live to a great age and if the food source is rich and diverse then a good yearly weight gain can be expected. Also, if she is the top predator then she has all the advantages. So why do we not see reported captures of these great creatures? Maybe it is because they are not specifically tracked down and fished for as much as other species? Or are they way too smart to make obvious mistakes, especially when you consider that a 9 lb eel of sixty years will not have got that old by being careless? In reality though what is a specimen eel for the British Isles?

What is a Specimen Eel?

Similar to other predatory species like perch and even chub, you must think outside the box when defining a specimen eel. We are not talking doubles, twenties, thirties, forties and beyond as we do with other freshwater predators like pike and catfish. No,

This 3 lb 4 oz specimen took a live skimmer bream for Steve Ormrod.

And another 3 lb 4 oz specimen for Steve Ormrod, this one falling to worms.

we are mainly looking at single-figure milestones. This may seem a bit puny compared to larger-growing predators, but do not let it put you off. Ounce for ounce, note not pounds, *Anguilla* is one of the hardest fighting freshwater fish you will come across in the British Isles. You will probably have come across 'boots' or 'boot laces', as we also affectionately call small eels in the 8 to 12 oz category, while coarse fishing with maggots. They do fight hard on 4 lb line and a match rod so just imagine a good 5 lb eel that is ten times the size of a boot? Even with good, strong tackle it will test your fish-playing skills to the limit.

So what do eel specialists consider a specimen to be? It may surprise you that anything over 3 lb is considered to be worthy of specimen status. You will get a decent fight off a 2 lb fish, and 3 lb fish are real battlers and a good achievement. You can then congratulate yourself on a successful eel season if you catch a 4 lb specimen. A 5 lb fish is not uncommon, but this is increasingly becoming a benchmark weight for big eels. If you are lucky enough to catch a 6 lb fish, it will be a hard to repeat catch. Eels of 7 lb are the stuff of legend, and to land an 8 lb, you will have to work really hard, be mentally dedicated and put in a lot of homework and night-hours. A fish of 9 lb upwards is exceptional and a rare catch indeed and you may even think you have fallen asleep during a slow night's sport and had the loveliest of dreams.

What is quite remarkable is the gap between what is considered a specimen eel, 3 lb, to the current British record of 11 lb 2 oz. Yes, 11 lb 2 oz, a difference of 8 lb or almost four times the body weight. To put this in perspective it is like comparing a pike of specimen size, usually 20 lb, and quadrupling it to 80 lb … if only! Let us briefly consider the history of British record eels. In 1922, Mr C Mitchell recorded an 8 lb 8 oz and in 1948 it was equalled by a Mr Ward. There was then a twenty-one year wait for a 2 oz increase by Alan Dart in 1969. Finally, the current British record is 11 lb 2 oz caught by Stephen Terry from a Hampshire water and this has now stood for almost thirty years. It certainly does makes you realise that eels of 8 lb and upwards are very difficult to purposely catch, this in turn reminding me of an eeling experience I will never forget.

Back in 1998, my eeling partner Eric 'the fish' Brown and I were feeling pretty good having conquered a water, landing fish to 3 lb 14 oz with plenty of good 'twos'. We were doing hit and run sessions as our work dictated the fishing hours. Turning up late afternoon, we would quickly secure some baits, then fish for the eels from 9 pm to 1 am. Later, when we felt we had got to grips with the water properly we had longer two or three day-and-night sessions.

On one of our hit and run sessions in June we were to fully experience this venue's eel potential. It had been a muggy day with high temperatures and no wind, with that heavy, suffocating cloud-cover making things sticky and humid. We were praying for a thunderstorm to break not least as they are very conducive to big eel fishing. Although there were a few rumbles over the Welsh mountains, we did not gain the treat.

Unusually, we had decided to fish one eel rod apiece earlier than usual at 8 pm, as it was thundery and not very bright. This season deadbaits ruled and we were each using freshly dispatched roach of about 3 inches in length. The first hour passed uneventfully, so we packed away the bit-bashing gear as we had plenty of baits to last us the session. We then swiftly placed the second baits in the chosen swims. Open water had proved to be the best place to fish the deadbaits which were enhanced by using large Drennan feeders crammed with mashed-up fish on a basic ledger rig. Eric had an old cast-iron mincer which we rather comically used to create our fish-mash with crumb and a little crushed hemp to give it 'fizz'.

We had just settled down in the chairs, ready for dark and the pregnant promise of action. The rod I had cast out earlier than normal suddenly started to literally shudder in the rests. The bite alarm did not sound at first, then gave out a few bleeps as the monkey-climber did a hypnotic dance up and down its stick. Soon the rod stopped quivering and peace resumed. 'What was that?' Eric said. Just as I replied 'dunno, maybe I'd better check the bait', the bobbin smacked up against the rod blank and the alarm screamed blue murder.

As we were having more hook-ups by striking as a run developed rather than waiting for a pause, I closed the bale and almost had the rod taken from my grip. I did not even get the chance to strike as the rod folded over. 'Fish on!' I exclaimed as the give away thump-thump action on the rod confirmed that it was an eel. By now the light was fading, but you could still see quite well. I managed to gain some sort of control and

Eric Brown and Steve Ormrod with some nice eels to almost 3 lb.

applied a bit of pressure to retrieve line before this eel headed straight for tree roots on the opposite bank. She then responded by coming to the surface, pulling against the pressure of my NW Kevlite rod and slowly taking line off the clutch. What we then experienced will haunt us forever. The eel was making large S-shaped boils out on the surface, with resulting bubbles and silt swirling around as if an aerator was in use. As I gained an inch of braid this fish would then take two back, such was its swaggering prowess. Things were going nowhere and Eric was fantasising about some huge 8 lb plus monster while I was sweating like a pig.

It was not to be though, as suddenly all went very slack and I looked at Eric in disbelief. A big lesson had been learned that evening; never again did we use the trusted 80 lb braid as hook links that this eel had cleverly sawn right through. We were converted to using soft-strand wire instead after that. We went home at 1 am, eel-less and with our tails firmly between our legs.

So, having perhaps missed my chance of an 8 lb eel, let us consider the possibilities of the 8 lb barrier being broken again. Since the late 1970s there have been quite a few big fish recorded in the 8 to 9 lb bracket. Indeed, large eels are probably caught regularly by specimen carp and tench hunters, but not being considered as 'target' quarry, they are returned unweighed and thus unrevealed. Having said that, in more recent times several monsters over 10 lb have broken the 'unreachable' double-figure barrier and made it into the angling press.

The waters with the greatest potential to produce a new record usually already have a history of big eels or have remained unfished for them. Even then, this is not a guarantee as most 'known' big-eel producing waters will receive specialist attention. Also, predatory eels can be catholic in their selection of food; they will eat almost anything. Interestingly, you see a lot of reports of big eels being caught in matches on carp poles using maggots and pastes. Similarly, carp and tench anglers catch big specimens on boilies and fishmeal-based pellets, this proving that a water unfished for specimen eels with specialist tactics holds a very good chance of one being caught 'by accident'. It really makes you think, especially when some are caught in broad daylight too.

Consequently, a commercial carp fishery that regularly sees lots of high-protein bait going in could well be a good bet for an exceptional eel. However, my money would lie with a small, unfished farmland pond or estate lake, rich in biodiversity of natural flora, fauna and stuffed with stunted rudd. It will have remained undisturbed and not been exposed to any leeching of artificial agricultural fertilisers. Well, we can all have our dreams! But more seriously you have to know where you are likely to catch a big eel and this is what I now turn to.

Location and Habitats

What types of venue then are most likely to hold large predatory eels? Several all-important features and biological factors must exist as a starting point. First, we need to narrow things down a bit because as I have already pointed out eels are everywhere; but it is the big barren females we want to target. The specimen hunter's largest dilemma is choosing a water that holds a worthy quarry which means it has specimens present and is not full of developing 'boots'. My advice would be to do some homework and exploratory visits to waters you consider potentially good for big eels. Concentrate on stillwaters like pits, lakes and large ponds that are in close proximity to rivers, streams, drains and canals. Do not discount more urban waters either, as suitable venues do not need to be out in the wilds of the countryside. Also look for 'prison' venues with steep banks making it more difficult for eels to leave.

I have already hinted at where a typical lair of a big eel might be, and there are various features to look for. These include large weedbeds and reedy areas, brickwork structures, bridges, tunnels, boathouses, fallen trees and root systems, overhanging shrub and tree cover, rocky ledges with crevices and so on. Deep troughs, islands and peninsulas in gravel pits are also worth a look. Even foreign objects like a shopping trolley in a canal can 'hold' a large eel. Drowned insects in margins, even small dead animals and birds, especially the windward banks that have food sources blown into them can be eel haunts. Then, again as mentioned earlier, there are the territorial patrol routes, not usually very far from an eel's lair. These can be on sloping banks, ledges, drop-offs, silt-bars, undercut banks, and even open water where prey is present. Eels also gravitate to seasonal spawning grounds of other fish species as they do love fish eggs. Silt beds, coloured water and fish activity also need to be considered. So there certainly are lots of things to look for.

Once the features are found there are then other factors to consider. Ask questions of any anglers fishing there; have they caught any eels, are they plagued by 'boots' at all? Discount any unlikely venues to bring the odds down. Waters with stunted prey fish shoals like small rudd, roach and perch are good targets. Are there other predators present like pike, catfish, zander, perch and even chub? Does the water home fish-eating birds like goosander, grey herons and the dreaded black plague, cormorants? They will also impact on available food sources and prey on eels too. Competition is an important factor to consider and will narrow down the chances of a really big eel residing in your chosen water. By recognising potential eel habitats and the correct water biology you will naturally have chosen a water to fish, even if it is by default.

The Eeling Calendar

Having selected our venue we now need to know when to go eeling. The earlier section on the eel's life cycle should already have given some good clues as to when to fish for big eels, but here I want to consider the yearly calendar and what potential each month holds for a big eel.

Late April is a good starting point for our calendar as it is when the eel migration starts; maternal eels get the urge to return to the sea. This is usually triggered by a rise in water temperature as the days get longer and the sun's effect is felt. Sport can be good with medium-sized fish being caught as they feed-up for their long journey. You may be lucky and catch a morphing 'silver'. The mass eel activity will arouse the larger 'barren' specimens too, making a good eel a possibility.   In May, water temperatures begin to rise considerably and other fish species start to spawn. This can be a good time to fish for eels as they can go on frenzied feeding spells, literally gorging themselves on fish eggs and hatching fry. All this gives the angler the chance to dust down the eel gear, gain some confidence and get back into the swing of predatory eel fishing. The main elver run also occurs during May and into June, but may start as early as April with high spring tides and end as late as October. Much depends on the 'drift timing' of the young eels returning from the Atlantic spawning grounds.

June, July and August are probably the best months for general eel fishing. The fish will be very active during the short, warm nights, and a variety of different-sized eels can be caught from two pounders up to the real biggies. Those hot, sticky nights with thunderstorms thrown in are optimum times for a good eel catch and should not be ignored. Picture the experience; getting soaked to the skin by big blobs of warm summer rain whilst pitting your skills against a hard-fighting eel lit up by the sudden flash of lightning. Then there is the rumble of thunder crashing all around soon afterwards as you unhook your prize; all this is magic and reminds me of one July night a few years ago.

It was 2002 there had been a very stormy day with heavy bursts of rain, thunder and lightning. This continued into the dark and was perfectly conducive for eel activity. At approximately 1 am I returned a 2 lb 8 oz fish caught on worms fished on the far bank. I settled back in the bivvy and fitfully dozed. At just gone 2 am the rain had abated, the air was still and smelt 'charged' from the storm. Mist rolled off the water's surface and I became aware of splashing sounds. I crept to the waterside and noticed the whole water was

Eric Brown with a nice Cheshire estate lake 3 lb 11 oz eel.

117

alive with small fish. There were literally hundreds of small roach and rudd cavorting in the top layers, probably enjoying the extra oxygen generated by the heavy rains. It really was an amazing sight and shortly afterwards an eel struck them leaving a sinuous fizz and boil on the surface.

A rod came quickly in, I scooped a few small lives, baited up and in they went amongst the fishy orgy. I purposely fished them up near the surface where the activity was as the eels were striking at the silhouettes above. But surprisingly, apart from a few 'liners', no action was had even though more eels were seen striking; it really was enough to drive you mad. I resorted to freelining a small livebait with a betalight for indication, but still had no luck. Soon the sky started to lighten up, the activity slowly abated and the eels went off for their daylight kip no doubt with full bellies. I was beaten by *Anguilla* yet again.

Moving to September and October, depending on the weather, they can also be good months to fish for big eels, especially if an Indian summer is on the cards. Water temperatures will still be high and the added advantage are the longer nights which means extended eel activity time and more chances of action.

In November, when things get a bit cooler, there is an excellent chance of a bigger eel as the smaller fish will in effect hibernate for the winter. Larger eels are better prepared for colder conditions having extra body mass and greater fat reserves which provides stamina to aid them in their search for food. A negative will be availability of bait sources because preyfish shoal up and do not feed as prolifically as in the summer. This is where being a good all-round angler comes into his own. You will also have to put up with long, cool runless nights, but if that bobbin and bite alarm goes and there are no pike in your water you could be going home with a big smile on your face.

As for December, January and February, it has to be said that although they are generally not considered eeling months, a lot of big predatory eels have been caught in these colder months. John Sidley used to purposely fish smaller deadbaits on one rod whilst pursuing pike, and he caught several 6 lb and 7 lb fish during this time of the year. My thoughts are that he probably fished them very close to likely eel lairs which he had sussed out during the summer. The fish would be semi-hibernating and he will have activated some interest in them to feed. We should also consider that with the advent of global warming we are experiencing much warmer winters which could therefore be good for eeling.

Finally we come to March and I have found it to be a good time to eel fish, especially if things have warmed up a bit. Similar to John Sidley, I will sometimes fish a small deadbait on one of the rods whilst pike fishing. This has the added bonus that it will be taken by a pike anyway and I have landed fish as big as 25 lb 8 lb (pike that is!). This seems to work especially well on slow-flowing waters for some reason. Maybe it is due to eels that have moved back into running waters and are feeding up prior to their journey to the sea. After all it does take them several weeks/months of feeding and morphing activity to prepare for their eventual migration.

The foregoing calendar indicates the importance of the weather in relation to eel fishing, and I must admit that during the colder months whilst pike fishing I take detailed notes on the weather as well as moon phases, pressure, high tides and the like, using all this to good effect when angling. You will be perhaps surprised to hear that I do not do the same with my specimen eeling nowadays. This was not always the case as during the late 1990s I set about gaining as much data as possible to see if there were any patterns I could use to good advantage. Amazingly, nothing correlated like it did with pike fishing. Into the new millennium and my approach was if I could get out eeling then I would do, whatever the weather was doing. Even so, there are specific factors that certainly cannot be ignored and in my view the major driver for eeling success is the correct water temperature. As it rises above 10° it is safe to say that eels, and their prey, will be active. Temperatures as high as 17° will see increased activity and as already mentioned thunderstorms are brilliant conditions for eeling, especially at night. The specimen eel angler who decides he does not want to fish due to the heavy downpours is missing what is probably *the* best conditions for a good catch and a big fish. It is only rain after all. Incidentally I also find that bright, moonlit nights, as long as the phase is on the fall, can be great for presenting surface-fished livebaits for eels.

Tackle, Tactics, Baits and Rigs

I now come to the practicalities of fishing for eels, namely the tackle, tactics, rigs and baits that are used. I deal with each in turn.

Tackle

If you fish for pike then you will not need to splash out on lots of new gear to fish for big eels. Pike gear is ideal and you will not be 'over-gunning' it. Rods should be through-action and not tippy; you want a forgiving action that will absorb the thumps of a side-winding fish, yet being beefy in the butt section to pile some power on to keep an eel under control. A test curve of 2.75 lb to 3 lb test is ideal, and do not be tempted to be 'sporting' and go any less than 2.5 lb; you will regret it. Normal medium-size baitrunners are fine and should be loaded with a good suspending braid of at least 24 lb. Mono is fine, but it offers far too much stretch for my liking, though admittedly it may be better to use heavy mono when fishing snags as braid can soon chafe and part.

Bite alarms should be such as front-end Delkims with lightweight drop-offs or monkey-climbers as indicators. I tend to use small bobbins off carp swingers and attach them with stainless ball chains to my banksticks. Too heavy a bobbin will see dropped runs on some waters. The same goes with baitrunners so fish 'open-bail' wherever possible.

For traces, wire is a must and I tend to use 20 lb coated, and I crimp rather than twist for eels. You may get away with a strong braid or quicksilver, but I would not risk it especially if a good fish is likely. Power swivels are a good idea and do not be afraid to 'build-in' as many swivels in your end rig as possible as it helps avoid braid twist resulting from the way an eel fights. Concerning hooks, I tend to standardise on a size 1 ESP Raptor, the big T whisker-barb variety, as they are perfect for most bait uses. Do not use hooks with large barbs and please do not use doubles or trebles for eel fishing as they cause untold damage and stress to the fish. Bombs tend to be lead-free pears or dumpies of 2 to 3 oz depending on distance and presentation. I sometimes use 'flattened' bombs if it is a silty bed as they sit flat and offer a good hold too.

Tactics

When it comes to tactics you need to be aware of such as weather and water conditions, how the eels are feeding, what their preferences are and so on; some of these issues are highlighted in the 'windy swim experience' below. In short, you need to act upon any clues that might be around; after all it is called good watercraft. For example, eels can change preferences sometimes by the hour, so you have to be prepared for some real surprises and adapt accordingly.

Night fishing has to be the key time to tempt the better eels because, as I said earlier, they are far more active during the hours of darkness. However, again as I said earlier, deep water in shade can be a good option during daytime. I have also mentioned lairs and patrol routes, so placing baits there can prove to be productive tactics. Margin fishing can be awesome, especially, as we will see, when there are massed fry shoals round. Remember that warmer temperatures will be higher in the shallower margins even on deeper venues so they should be targeted.

If you are fishing a new venue for the first time, you need to be very flexible in your approach. Make sure there are plenty of different rigs and baits to try out and experiment with. For instance, if allowed I would fish with three rods. To begin with, on the first rod I would fish a big bunch of lobworms, on the second I would have a freshly dispatched small coarse deadbait, and on the third I would have a small live-bait. By using different presentations and fishing to several features you will soon find out where the eels hunt and what bait preferences they have. If one bait/rig/tactic out-fishes the others then apply it to all three rods and stick with it until the eels decide to change the rules. If things are slow-going, it is time to experiment and make changes. For instance, alter a deadbait fished 'hard-on' the bottom to one that is popped-up or suspended. Or try a whole deadbait with just its head removed, or a bigger bait cut in half. Then you should re-present these different baits and rigs in a variety of swims and features. It is also advisable to strike at the smallest indication of a bite as eels do not tend to 'run' the same from the margins as they do in deeper, open water. For example, they may well engulf your offering on the spot and if you do not strike early it can lead to unnecessary deep-hooking.

Groundbaiting with a fishmeal-based crumb mix laced with scalded maggots or tinned tuna/catmeat can be a good way to keep eels in your swim vicinity over longer periods. Adding a bit of crushed hemp will give it 'fizz'. All this can gain the eels' confidence leading to confident runs. A lonely offering often results in an eel 'smash, grab and run' to its lair before another eel gets the chance to take the opportunity. Swimfeeders can also be used instead of a bomb and these can be packed with 'eel mash' consisting of freshly chopped up coarse fish or seabaits and/or some of the above ingredients. The advantage with this is that it presents a small pocket of scent right by your hookbait.

Baits and Rigs

In dealing with baits and rigs, here I give an overview of the main baits and their general presentation before describing some successful rigs in more detail.

Worms and slugs can be presented ledgered hard on the bottom, popped up off-bottom or suspended on a paternoster. Always nip the tip off the heads of worms so they cannot burrow into the silt and this also releases scent. Do not be afraid to fish as many as six large lobworms at once though you must make sure your hook point is not masked. You may well get them nibbled by other 'nuisance' species, and if this is a real problem you could fish them on a suspended rig well above the bottom. Worms can be held on the hook by small pieces of elastic band. If there are plenty of overhanging bushes and shrubs by the bankside and an abundance of slugs, try fishing one on a large single hook right below the vegetation in the margins. Eels love slugs and will often look for them here. Furthermore, there is no need for a complex rig, with a trace and a few swan-shot to pin it down being ideal.

As with worms, fish deadbaits can be presented ledgered hard on the bottom, popped up off-bottom or suspended on a paternoster. They can be fished whole, halved, or my favourite, with the head neatly cut off and tailfins snipped down to aid hook-ups.

Roach can be great baits for eels – this 6 oz fish has had a close encounter with a predatory eel.

Freshly caught and killed coarse baits are best; gudgeon are excellent, though small roach, rudd, dace, bleak and perch are winners too. I have used small skimmers in the past, but find their deep body profile a disadvantage in terms of actually hooking eels. Importantly do not be tempted to use fish that may have died in your keep-net or bucket. Freshly dispatched fish are certainly the best bet though you must take care not to let neighbouring pleasure anglers witness it as they may well get a bit upset. Avoid using frozen fish too as I have found them to be virtually useless; although small sea baits like anchovies and sprats have accounted for some good fish for others, I have never had success on them. Rotting or 'off' baits are also not very effective and they can lead to frustration when an eel turns to its 'bite and spin' mode of corpse feeding; all you will retrieve is a well-chewed bait. Small sections of lamprey can be killers on certain waters, as can eel 'boot' sections as big eels are cannibalistic.

Size of bait will ultimately depend on the eel potential. As a rough guide I stick with whole 3 to 4 inch baits and 5 to 6 inch halved baits to begin with. If you miss runs downsize your baits to suite. Do not be afraid to try out larger baits though as they may single out a better sized eel and also lessen the attention of smaller ones. Although I would not expect too many runs on them, if you do get a take your heart will skip a beat or two. And a final tip is to give your deadbaits a few neat stabs with a sharp knife to release blood and juices; remember that eels hunt mainly by scent location.

When it comes to coarse livebaits you must never move live fish from one venue to another. You do not want to risk spreading disease, so always catch and use livebaits at the venue being fished. You must also be sure that livebaiting is allowed on your venue. When it comes to species, size and presentation, basically the same applies as with dead-baits. However, treat your lives with care and hook them up in a bucket and get them into the water immediately so as to minimise damage and stress so they will present as a livelier, more tempting target. If you can only catch very small fish you can even put two or three on the same hook. Always put a 'bait-saver', such as a small piece of elastic band, over your hook to stop the bait either wriggling off or being snatched off by an eel. If you like to watch a float a great way to present lives is to free roam them beneath a small balsa float with a betalight inserted in the tip. You may get a bit goggle-eyed watching it for too long in the dark, but it does create a buzz when a take occurs.

Takes on suspended lives can be savage but do not be tempted to strike at the first run. Remember the eel's attack profile from earlier; it will disable a victim first then return to some easy pickings. What happens is that the eel hits the bait, disabling it with the initial indication being a fast run with a fallen drop-off. The 'run' will then slow but in fact it is the livebait continuing it, not the eel itself. While all this is happening I quickly tighten the braid up to the bobbin again. Meanwhile the eel spins round to retrieve its wounded victim and a more positive, second run occurs; this is the time to strike as the eel makes off with its meal. It is a very successful technique that, after a bit of practice, you will soon have down to a fine art. In passing, always carefully check any decent bite indications with lives, especially if ledgering them as they may have been snatched off the hook by a larger fish, or mauled by a smaller one.

Having looked at deadbaits and livebaits, it reminds me of another memorable eeling occurrence, namely the aforementioned 'windy swim experience'. It relates to one particular two night session from 2000 which saw some amazing revelations in relation to eel habits and how I reacted to them. My first night was reasonably successful, a couple of fish to 2 lb plus on live gudgeon which were caught on the whip the same evening. The night in question had been very still and sticky, much like it had been all week, with 90° F temperatures during the daytime. The following day was not so hot and a moderate, coolish south-easterly wind put some badly needed oxygen into the water. The gudgeon obliged once more, so securing baits for the night ahead. I noticed that the wind was blowing directly into another favourite swim, so I decided to 'up-sticks' and recamp in that very swim for the second night.

Night fell and the eel action started with a few runs to lives on the CD rig (see below) with baits set mid-water but all were missed. This was very frustrating as the takes were confident. I concluded that as the bobbins were only set light, some were possibly caused by the live gudgeon trying to get away from the marauding eels, thus giving what seemed like a run. In addition, the baits were coming back unharmed, an unusual occurrence for a dropped run from a predatory eel. I tried setting the bobbins tighter so as to eliminate false runs but I was still missing them when the baits were reeled in. This is not that unusual as any big eel angler will tell you that you can miss four out of every five runs at times.

Steve Ormrod and a lovely 3 lb plus eel that took a half gudgeon on the CD rig.

Even so the eels were obviously up for it good style and with the wind still pushing into the swim, I thought 'better get it sorted Stevie or you're gonna miss out here!' Suddenly, after retrieving a mangled gudgeon from a screaming run, I had what can only be described as a desperate surge of inspiration. Although the moonlight convinced me that sub-surface lives would be the best bet, I made the decision to do the opposite and fish one rod with a deadbait just off-bottom. In any case the swim was only 5 ft deep so there was no great depth to worry about. I trimmed the now dead gudgeon to a tail section and quickly adjusted the float's stop-knots on the CD rig so the bait would be presented just off the bottom and recast it to the same spot. The bait was taken as I was clipping on the bobbin and led to a very good 3 lb 12 oz fish that put up a hell of a scrap.

The rest of that night was more or less a blur with eight fish landed to 4 lb 10 oz, the latter being one of the hardest fighting fish I have ever caught. I hate to think how many I missed from sheer fatigue due to lack of sleep and lost count of the runs at about midnight. All of these takes came on a halved freshly-killed gudgeon with both heads or tails being equally successful. Incredibly lives were ignored in preference to these dead halves. As I ran out of live gudgeon in the dawning hours I resorted to using gudgeon deadbaits which I had saved from the day before just in case I ran out. But these older baits went untouched with seemingly the freshness factor being the key to the success. I have heard that gudgeon are full of amino acids and maybe these were no longer effective on the slightly older baits. In any case, this episode proved to me that what works on one night can suddenly be useless the next, but that by being resourceful and in effect experimenting success can be achieved. Also, the change of swim to where food was being deposited by the prevailing wind proved to be a worthwhile gamble.

Finally in relation to baits, other possible ones that I have come across being used include: pig's liver 'flappers', that is slim slices; chicken entrails though these have been used mainly as groundbait and are not for the faint hearted; squid as per for catfish but smaller samples; and king prawns.

Turning to rigs, there are two successful eel rigs that I will now describe in more detail. First, there is the 'CD' paternoster rig. This has to be my favourite big eel fishing rig as it is so adaptable and is free-running thereby offering little resistance to a spooky eel. It was originally devised by Vic Bellars and adapted by Colin Dyson, two of my fishing heroes. As indicated, it can be used to present any baits in a variety of presentations whether it be just off the bottom, mid-water or near the surface. This is perfect if you need to adapt your tactics quickly and avoids time wasting rig changes, especially so when it is dark. Basically, it is a paternoster rig with the float sitting ahead of the baited trace suspending it at whatever depth is required, this being determined by the length of bomb-tail you use; for example, short for near the bottom and long for near the surface. A big, buoyant sub-surface float offers good tension to your braid, so giving superb bite indication and it also gives the bait some 'movement' as it will sway in the undertow or wind-chop. Takes on this rig are supremely confident and what is more it is a very easy rig to make up.

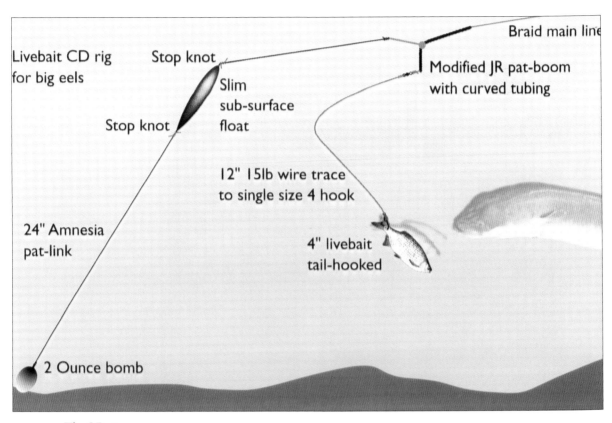

Livebait CD rig for big eels

Stop knot

Stop knot

Slim sub-surface float

Braid main line

Modified JR pat-boom with curved tubing

12" 15lb wire trace to single size 4 hook

24" Amnesia pat-link

4" livebait tail-hooked

2 Ounce bomb

The CD rig.

Second, there is the Sidley ledger rig, another legendary rig made famous by its creator, the late John Sidley. It is devised for ledgering in silty or snaggy swims. Basically, it is a free-running ledger rig that has a buoyant ledger 'stem' attached to the bomb to keep your braid up above any silt-beds. The ledger stem has a weak mono link within it so if you get snagged-up a break is possible. By using a small amnesia up-trace you can make good distance casts as it absorbs the shock, this ensuring your bait stays on the hook. It is another easy-to-make rig too.

When it comes to other rig considerations, mention must be made of anti-gorge rigs. Eels can be very greedy and no matter how quickly you strike a bite indication, deep-hooking can be a real problem. This is especially so when you consider the small 'working area' you have in an eel's throat for unhooking purposes. However, a lot can be done to stop an eel swallowing baits too deeply. I came up with two end rigs to avoid this, namely the crossbar and poly-ball. They may seem a bit crude, but eels seem unaffected by them once on the feed and they work very well. Basically, the crossbar jams across the eels jaws, stopping it from taking a bait any deeper, the poly-ball does a similar job as it cannot be swallowed. It also acts as a built-in bait popper too if you need to present a bait off-bottom. By seeing where the devices are, you have an instant guide to where your hook will be too.

I have had mixed success with hair-rigs and if I am really honest they have not put any extra fish on the bank for all the effort required in setting them up. One very clever version was given to me by Peter Waterfield who in my view is a 'thinking' predator angler. He devised a hair-rig which utilised clothing tags used in the shops to attach labels. You need a special tag gun to 'fire' the tags through baits and it may be a bit fiddly but with practice it gives a very neat presentation and keeps your bait lively.

I have had mixed success with bolt rigs, their advantage being that they avoid deep-hooking but the disadvantage is that they are not resistance-free which is often needed with shy fish.

Finally, there is the medusa rig which was first devised for carp fishing. It is basically

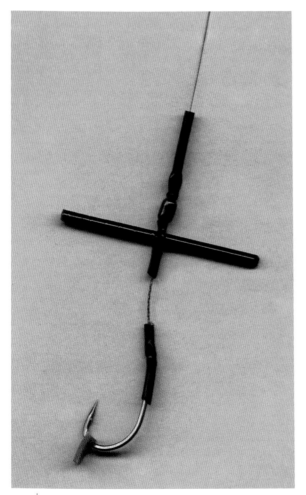

The crossbar anti-gorge rig.

The poly-ball anti-gorge rig.

a bait-popper tied with a hair off the hook, and large 'gozzer' maggots are then superglued one at a time to the popper. For eels it can be scaled down and although I have never used it I know some anglers who have done well with it. My concerns are obviously environmental as it is using glue, and also using maggots will attract attention from nuisance species giving you false runs and nibbled baits.

To finish on rigs, I always consider alternatives and try to be creative, incidentally both with baits as well as rigs, as even a small adjustment or modification could make all the difference.

Hooking, Playing and Netting

I now come to hooking, playing and netting a specimen eel. The most important consideration whilst big eel fishing is to remember to strike early and avoid deep-hooking as it can be a real eel killer. My key advice is to adopt a 'hit and hold' approach. So long as your wire, swivels, links and braid are strong and up to the job, there is no way you should suffer any breaks. I prefer to play an eel on a tight clutch, rather than backwind as this gives them too much freedom to get up to their many tricks. As mentioned earlier, they can swim forwards, backwards and sideways. They have a fantastically adapted tool in their muscular tail which acts as a giant 'finger' as it probes for snag-holds and wraps around sunken branches, roots and rocks, all of which test your reactions and ability to keep in control. I set my clutch more or less as normal to just above the breaking point of my braid which admittedly is quite tight.

Let me run through a typical scenario from a run in open water to netting. First, place your landing net close to the waterside and submerge the mesh in the margins if possible. Pick up the rod and quickly strip off a yard or so of free braid, engage the bail arm and wait until the braid tightens to the rod. All you need to do then is make a smooth sweep upwards and away from the run direction. This should see the eel firmly hooked and then you should keep your rod elevated, with a healthy bend in it; do not relinquish the pressure or level it to give any slack as you will lose your fish. Use the hit and hold method by not allowing the eel to gain any braid if possible. Your rod will bang up and down, this being caused by the eel's thrashing 'side-to-side' fighting action. She twists in an 'S' motion, the 'thump' comes at the end of each of the sideways twists and applies considerable force, this being how she loosens the hook-hold by making it slacker in her jaw. The real trick is not to play an eel too long and get her to the net as soon as possible. I am afraid this really is no place for a 'sporting' fight.

I will often jam my rod butt against my thigh for leverage and grip the bottom section of blank with my left hand rather than the upper handle as it controls lunges better. I release the pressure and wind the reel handle to quickly gain extra braid as appropriate. My other hand covers the reel and I use my forefinger and thumb to grip the spool, which allows me to give braid under complete control. Do not just let an eel pull braid off the spool more or less as it wishes, and control sudden lunges by lowering

127

your rod tip a little, so giving a few inches rather than a foot or so. It is also important to watch for sudden 'flying surges' to left or right and the unexpected tail-walk along the surface; if given a chance she will do it.

Once you are near the bankside you will be glad you positioned the net first. Any messing about trying to find the net and releasing tension on the fish will see it quickly get away. As the eel comes within netting range, I tend to kneel down and only when I know I can swiftly draw the fish over the net in one smooth motion will I grab the net with my left hand. Then there is the tricky bit of keeping the pressure on and getting the eel's head out of the water, which disorientates her and makes netting easier. Then draw her quickly over the net, making sure her head comes a foot over the spreader block, and swiftly lift the net in one go. The eel should just slide in. Do not 'stab' at the fish with the net as it will get free. A big eel will also use its tail to good effect by gripping the edge of your net rim, this allowing her to swim backwards out of the net leaving your hook in the rim. Finally, after the netting do not be tempted to unclip your trace at the waterside, instead take everything well onto dry land to your unhooking mat.

Handling, Weighing and Photography

The best idea is to prepare your unhooking area well before dark by placing the unhooking mat on a flat area of grass and pinning it down with pegs. A rag, forceps, snips, weighing bag and scales should all be handy. I also use a plastic wallpaper bag that the big stores provide, this being perfect for long, slim objects like wallpaper rolls and eels alike. After a bit of use they can be discarded and importantly they remove very little eel slime if wetted first. Another advantage is that they have large, centred handles thereby making weighing very simple.

So, we have the fish on the mat and it should then be wrapped in the net folds while a rag is placed over her head, the ensuing darkness helping to subdue her. Then unclip the trace and get the rod out of harm's way, this being especially important because it will be dark and very easy to stand on. What follows depends on how lively your eel is, as well as your confidence which in turn comes with experience.

Fortunately, bigger fish are far easier to unhook than smaller boots. Keep the eel in your landing net with the net folds around its tail and lower body coils. Then raise its head with the trace but do not be heavy-handed as eels tend to struggle the more pressure you apply. Grip the hook shank with the forceps and give a sharp flick of the wrist which should do the job nicely. Do not ever put your finger in a predatory eel's mouth however easy it may seem to unhook; she has very powerful jaws with an incredible pounds per inch pressure for her size. If the hook is well back in the eels throat be careful as all her vital organs like heart and liver are situated near this area. If the hook is out of sight, snip off the trace as close to the gullet opening as possible; amazingly, eels can regurgitate an out-of-sight hook. If I am unfortunate in having a deeply-hooked fish, I put it in the keep-net until daybreak. Again it is amazing how they get rid of the hook and even if they have not completely done this, often you will find it has moved into the mouth cavity for easy removal. Do not on any account go digging around as you will finish up with one dead eel.

Once unhooked, I quickly put the eel in the wallpaper bag and give it a weighing. If it is less than 3 lb I usually return it there and then. All you need to do is to pop the eel's head out the bag and let it slither into the margins. If it is over 3 lb and I want a photograph, I will retain the eel until daybreak, which in summer is not long. Ideally use a large diameter keep-net with decent-sized knotless mesh, avoiding micro-mesh as there needs to be maximum water flow through it. The net should be at least 16 ft long to give the eel room to move around. Square profile nets designed for bream are ideally suited. Make sure the keep-net sits in the deepest margin water as possible and

has a decent end weight to keep the rungs upright. Secure it well to the bank with a powerdrive bankstick. Lastly, and most importantly, close the top mesh section with a piece of string because if you do not the eel will slither up the net and out of the opening even if it is elevated.

Why retain the eel and not photograph it after unhooking? Well, in the first place the photographing is far easier in daylight, but more importantly it gives your fish time to recover. Remember the eel will be stressed out enough having been hauled from her habitat, unhooked and weighed. It takes time and patience to photograph eels properly, so let them rest before doing it. Photographing eels is made far easier if you prepare your handling area well. When you have enough available light to work, reel in your rods and start the photography process. You could use a shallow bucket to put the eel in, which allows it to wriggle, but does not let it get away. I well recall some

Steve Richardson with a 4 lb 9 oz eel from North Yorkshire.

comical episodes of eels writhing off into the undergrowth, for example. But apart from a bucket I prefer using an inflatable unhooking mat with high sides that are dampened lightly. I make a 2 inch deep groove in nearby soft earth and lay the unhooking mat over it. I then form a gully down the middle of the mat by pushing it down into the groove and wetting it well. The eel is then laid in the gully this supporting the whole body length and actually calming and subduing it. Do not use newspaper to try and do this; it is a fallacy that you should try this not least as it removes too much of the eel's protective slime.

Once the eel is in place perhaps you need to stroke it with wetted hands. The technique is quite simple in that you turn the eel on its side, holding its body firmly but not tightly with one hand. Do not hold it near the base of the skull though as this will suffocate it as well as risking damage to vital organs, so hold it a few inches lower down the body instead. With the other wetted hand gently stroke the body head to tail for several minutes. This can be fun depending how lively your eel is and the length of stroking time will be dictated by it. However, after a while you will feel your eel relax enough to hold it up to pose for a few snaps. If the eel becomes active again, do not wrestle with it; simply lay it down and start again. Trust me, it will work eventually and with practice you will become quite the snake charmer. The photos can then be taken; I use a small digital camera on a tripod that is set to capture myself and the fish as close as possible. The beauty with digital, of course, is that you can take lots of pictures and get a good result.

Some specimen 'snake-charmed' eels.

Steve Ormrod with a recent 2 lb 10 oz Lakeland eel caught while pike fishing.

Current Eel Concerns

Before concluding, as many readers will be aware, over the last couple of decades there have been serious concerns about a dramatic decline in eel stocks. The number of juvenile eels returning to our rivers has fallen to just one per cent of historic levels and there are very real concerns that they could be extinct in our waters within the next ten years or so. The precise reasons for this decline are presently unclear but there are a number of inter-related factors to note. First, there are cyclic and worldwide climatic changes leading to changes in ocean currents which affect successful migration to target habitats and the natural variation in numbers of eels. Second, over-fishing of arriving elvers and of eels returning to the sea to spawn, both for human consumption, has unfortunately helped to speed up their decline. It must be remembered that eels are still caught by netsmen for the table in England and that at present there is no limit on the quantities involved. Third, there is the loss and/or degradation of suitable freshwater habitats. For example, there is the accumulation of agricultural chemicals leeching into the water systems, along with others such as chemicals used to produce

131

non-stick and water-repellent coatings commonly known as 'PFCS'. In relation to this Greenpeace recently published their considerable findings on the effects these chemicals have by accumulating in fishes' livers, especially eels. Finally, but certainly not least, there are concerns about eels being infected by swim-bladder parasites, *anguillicola*, as well as the impact of other invasive/non-indigenous species which negatively impact on eels.

The 'powers that be' have certainly begun to recognise the seriousness of the problem facing eels and other endangered species. Consequently we have, for instance, the United Nations Convention on International Trade in Endangered Species of Wild Flora and Fauna. This has recently acknowledged the need for preservation aims and the introduction of effective control and conservation measures. In the long term perhaps the only manageable solution is the restoration of our rivers in accordance with the Water Framework Directive of the European Union; after all rivers act as vital ecological corridors. Closer to home, the Environment Agency is considering ways to secure a brighter future for *Anguilla* by the implementation of an eel management plan. Simple measures, like putting structures in place to help eels get past weirs and installing special traps to check upstream migrating elver numbers are being proposed.

The message from the above is to treat eels with the utmost respect and return them alive and well. In the not too distant future, it would be sad if all we could say was something along the lines of the rather sad refrain 'eels, I remember fishing for them'.

Conclusion

Eels then are certainly a worthy target for freshwater predator and specimen anglers. My firm belief is that if you need a fresh predator challenge, then you should certainly give big eel fishing a go. If you fish for pike or even catfish, apart from making up a few rigs and traces, you basically have all the gear you need. If you dislike night fishing you could always look at fishing a venue that gets little sunlight and fish on an overcast, preferably stormy day. You may be pleasantly surprised at how addictive the search for that elusive 5 lb plus specimen gets; and good luck in your endeavours if you do take up the challenge. Last, but certainly not least, I would urge us all to 'salute *Anguilla*' and let us hope that, despite some comments in the last section, we will be fishing for eels for many years to come.

5
Perch
Mark Barrett

I imagine the perch, *Perca fluviatilis*, is a fish that just about every angler who has ever wielded a rod in freshwater has encountered at some time. This is usually in its smaller form, when a worm or maggot, probably intended for something else, has been snaffled by this greedy predator. I certainly know that it was the first fish that I ever encountered, and for many anglers it stays really just that, a fish of one's youth; the proud, greedy, bait robber that was also a fish to be handled with care lest you lost a finger.

However, there is so much more to the perch than the delinquent juveniles. As Dick Walker said of perch, 'they are the biggest of all the fish'. What was meant by this on-the-face-of-it illogical statement, was that somewhere within the perch's life it metamorphoses into a swaggering football of a fish. Without doubt this will always lead the angler to question both its weight and how this fish could be from the same gene pool as the bait robbers with which he/she had become accustomed. Therein lies the essence of Dick's statement. It is not in pure physical size that the perch is the biggest, but in the transformation that occurs in the mind's eye as the angler turns from youth to adulthood.

Looking at my own perch fishing and the place that perch fishing has within the British Isles, I guess that there are two differences of opinion. Whilst I am a mad keen perch angler, the general population of the freshwater angling world does not seem to hold perch in such high esteem. Admittedly there may be a deal of fondness, but there is not the reverence for other species such as carp as occurs in England in particular. Perhaps though there is something of a sea change happening and much of the reason for this, for more anglers setting out their stall to catch perch, is the increasing availability of the species again. Though a resilient fish on the whole, the perch population of England in particular went through a massive decline when perch disease swept across the country in the 1960s and 1970s. Fortunately, I was not around at the time to witness what would have been the heart-breaking sight of hundreds upon hundreds of dead or dying perch being washed ashore as the disease decimated the species. My father tells of a trip around one of the London reservoirs during this period, and as far as the eye could see the margins of the reservoir were littered with dead perch. That the outbreak was cataclysmic for the overall perch population there can be no doubt, but nature is rarely so cruel as to completely destroy a species. Consequently, from the tiny pockets of perch that remained an increase in numbers ensued, an increase that eventually led to the perch once again becoming a frequent visitor to the nets of anglers throughout the land. If truth be told, this recovery took the species into areas where they were previously unheard of, as the angling world of the 1960s and 1970s changed irrevocably. Where once the perch was just a part of the predatory biomass, the advent of commercial fisheries, again in England in particular, has seen it become the only predator in these incredibly rich environments. This has meant the weight of the fish increase year on year to weights that would have been seen as unobtainable in the last century. To paraphrase another famous quote, this time from Prime Minister Harold MacMillan, for the perch fisher 'you've never had it so good'.

Yet despite this increase in habitat, population and size, the actual act of perch fishing still remains somewhat simple, and possibly from a bygone age. Though the elements that make up our perch tackle may have moved with the times, carbon rods replacing cane, fixed spool reels replacing pin at least for most parts, the methods that we employ today would not seem too alien to anglers from time passed by. Not least the baits with which we catch these modern perch owe nothing to modern technology. The humble lawn obtained lobworm will still catch many perch, from the delinquents to the queens, but even so the best bait of all for those bigger fish still remains the hapless smaller fish of our rivers and lakes. For those bigger fish, those biggest of all fish, are without doubt an extremely efficient predator.

Perch fishing has changed relatively little over the years; here are a brace of two pounders caught by Mark Barrett from a tiny river.

Perch are very efficient predators; Mark Barrett with a 2 lb 14 oz fish which took a livebait trotted from a boat.

So what of the perch itself, its life, make up and its habits? The answers to such questions are important, as to really excel at catching any fish you need to know, for instance, why that fish does what it does, and how the seasons and the water conditions change its willingness to feed. In what follows I address such issues, beginning with a discussion of perch and what we know about their lives and habitat, before turning to actually fishing for them. This includes location of perch and the timing, or when to go if you will, of those perch fishing sessions. Tackle and bait, including artificials, are then dealt with before I look at the actual methods of catching them including some perch fishing stories. As indicated, all this relates to my own perch fishing which is mainly based on the rivers, drains and stillwaters of eastern England, though nonetheless applicable to elsewhere in the British Isles. As a contrast however, this chapter then looks at canal perching particularly in north-west England, this being where Brian Steele has caught many specimen sized perch. Finally, before concluding I recall a great perch fishing session which led to the capture of an especially memorable fish.

Lives and Habitat

Perch have one of the most wide and diverse geographic spreads of all coarse fish species in the British Isles. From the tiniest of farm ponds, through such as rivers and canals, to the mightiest of Scottish lochs and Irish loughs, as well as the lakes of Wales, you will find perch. In fact, even on waters where there are no records of perch being stocked, they still find a way in via, for example, the various inlets into the water concerned or by anglers secretly introducing them.

They are handsome fish which do not really change much during their life as regards colouring or patterning, though the vivid camouflage stripes that often lead to the nickname of 'sergeants' or 'dandies', do tend to grow less pronounced with age. The most noticeable feature of the perch though is their spiny dorsal fin, as well as their very large mouth especially when this is compared to their body size. It is worth noting that this spiny dorsal is a common feature of the *perca* family, other members being zander and bass.

Perch then are one of the first fish to spawn in our fishing year, usually engaging in the annual ritual anywhere between March and April depending upon water temperature. The females lay millions of eggs and will start showing signs of this from February onwards as they put on weight and increase in size. As with all predators, once spawning has taken place the adult fish go on somewhat of a feeding spree to regain the weight and condition lost in the actual spawning process. Certainly no small fish or invertebrate is safe at this time, including their own young, hence the need, of course, for many millions of eggs.

Meanwhile, the tiny perch will, as with any fry, feed on micro-organisms until they reach a size when they can switch to small invertebrate life and eventually onto little prey fish. It is now generally accepted that the timing of this switch will eventually determine the perch's eventual size, the earliest switchers going on to be the bigger fish. Unfortunately not all rivers, lakes or stillwaters more generally will grow perch to very large sizes, though only the poorest of waters are likely not to grow fish to the 2 lb mark. Certain factors affect the growth rates of perch, the most obvious one being the availability of food. Although they are rather catholic in their tastes and will eat virtually anything in their lifetime, an abundance of a ready food source will always be an instrumental factor in allowing fish to reach their optimum size. Nowhere has this been better illustrated in recent years than in the perch of the upper Great Ouse. Here the perch have waxed fat on a diet of American signal crayfish. These crayfish have been a very bad impact on the native crayfish and on our waters in general, but they have had a positive effect on the ultimate size that the Great Ouse perch have reached. How perch actually manage to tackle these crays has always been open to conjecture, especially as they are quite formidable looking creatures reminiscent of small lobsters. The overriding strength of opinion seems to be that the fish probably take them when they are in the 'peeler' stage. Just like crabs and other invertebrates, crayfish are only able to grow by periodically shedding their outer casing. When they have done so, for a short period of time they are soft skinned and during this period they are extremely vulnerable to being eaten. Certainly the evidence is that perch do eat crayfish; often when they are caught they regurgitate parts from them. Without the pharyngeal teeth that cyprinid species such as chub and carp have in their throats, it seems unlikely that perch simply crush the crays as the cyprinids do. My view is certainly that the 'peeler' theory does seem plausible, and surely as crayfish are now endemic on many waters it is naive to expect that perch would not take advantage of an extremely available food source.

Here it is also important to note that perch are extremely mobile hunters, feeding mainly by sight. To enable the perch to do this effectively it has an anatomy that sets it aside from most other species. First, its manoeuvrability is achieved by its slightly unusual fin placement. On most species of fish the pelvic fins are roughly placed around the middle of the fish's body. However on the perch, as well as other members of the *perca* family, the pelvic fins are far closer to the head of the fish and this, along with the fins by the gill plate, allow it to turn and change direction very quickly. In addition, the perch has a double dorsal fin, which again increases the fin area to allow for rapid changes of direction. It also has exceptionally good eyesight like most

Big perch – here is Richard Scott with a 3 lb specimen – seem to be increasing on the Great Ouse as a result of feeding on signal crayfish.

predators and this enables them to see well for longer even into quite low light levels. This exceptional eyesight also enables it to spot the prey and get into position for the hunt before the prey is aware of its presence. Finally, as stated, perch have an extremely large mouth compared to the size of its body and this is used to engulf prey fish on the move, in effect almost vacuuming them in headfirst.

To digress a little, I used to keep perch in an aquarium and watched them feed on live prey and I am sure this has subsequently helped me in my perching. Thus, when a prey fish was spotted the perch would move close up quite slowly before launching itself. With smaller prey fish the perch would accelerate alongside the prey before turning and engulfing the fish headfirst. With bigger prey fish, the perch first attacks from behind, nipping at the rear end, particularly at the tail fins and the vent area and ventral fin. Eventually the prey fish would be damaged to a point where it was virtually disabled, whereupon it was taken head first and then swallowed over the course of time dependent upon size.

So knowing what we do about perch, what can we use from that to help us catch them? Bearing in mind the foregoing, perhaps one obvious point is that they like live fish so surely livebaiting can be key to catching them. This is certainly so and is something I certainly return to. Another is that perch are at their biggest weight around springtime. This effectively makes this the best time to catch the biggest specimens even though there is a problem as from 14 March the river season comes to an end for three months. This means that the bigger fish will have to be targeted in stillwaters. Knowing that perch are indeed present is obviously the first step but, taking things onto the next level, one has to know where those perch will actually be on any particular water. This is likely to be the dividing line between success and failure, so locating perch, as well as timing our sessions, are key factors.

Location

If there is one thing that draws perch like a magnet it is some form of structure within the water, be it man-made or natural. Places like mooring jetties, bridges, old walls, moored boats and lock gates are all structures that attract perch. Actually, my favourite of all perch spots are those landing or mooring jetties that are made up of old scaffold poles and boards that are out into the flow of a river. These offer perch absolutely everything that they require: a place from which to avoid overhead predation, a hideout from which to attack the prey fish that are also invariably drawn to such structures, and a lower light level something which the perch prefer for hunting. Numerous catches of good perch from such places have been made, including my personal best perch, but in reality anything that offers the perch a hideout will have its perch populations. I have seen them in some of the weirdest spots on a river, drawn to these because they offer a sense of security. Indeed, in my aquarium there was a length of drainpipe and the perch would very rarely leave the immediate vicinity of that pipe in daylight hours. But as the light faded they would bristle and emerge to feed, before heading back after dark.

Perch territory: structures such as lock gates and boats attract perch.

However, not every water has man-made structures to hold perch and so we also need to consider the sorts of natural cover that they prefer. Reed beds are a very consistent holder of perch. Here the fish can get right in amongst the reed stems, their striped camouflage holding them in good stead for avoiding detection from hunter and prey alike. If the reed beds are also breaking the flow of the river current, then so much the better. Perch also like to hold up in the slacker water and at the extreme margins. It is no real surprise why, as these areas are also favoured by the very small prey fish that make up a large percentage of their diet.

Deep holes in the river or lake also hold perch. Not only are such places very good ambush spots from which to attack the prey, but again they also offer lower light levels. Very much the same can be said for overhanging trees which are regular perch hang outs, particularly those that are close to the current, or those that overhang enough to form rafts where washed down detritus collects. Such areas are usually good for a number of different river species, but perch count them as a particular favourite.

Another factor that determines where perch reside is the availability of food. Though they are a rather more mobile hunter than pike for example, they still will not stray too far from where prey fish are. At times this can mean they migrate to different areas of the lake or river at particular times of the year. In the summer the prey fish are likely to be pretty well spread out, with an awful lot of the small fry taking up residence in the warmer, shallow water. It is the reverse come the depths of winter as these same small fry will most likely be in the deeper water in a lake, or in an area that offers them protection from the floodwater in a river.

Not all waters, thankfully, suffer from the plague of signal crayfish that the Great Ouse does, and yet they still manage to throw up very big perch. On these rivers the food source will be of a more natural variety so what we are looking for here is a very healthy population of small prey species, such as roach, bleak, gudgeon, chub, dace and minnows. To grow to a very large size, a perch will almost certainly be exclusively predatory, so the presence of such prey fish certainly helps in this regard.

Staying with small prey fish for a moment, if they also coincide with perch being the only predators within the aquatic environment then this can lead to the perch growing very large indeed. This is evidenced by the new, booming areas for perch fishing, namely commercial fisheries. Mistakenly, these waters do not tend to be stocked with any other predatory fish apart from perch. For some reason many anglers do not seem to see perch as predators, perhaps because it is quite rare to have them grabbing fish as they are being reeled in. Whatever the reason, on such waters the perch are pretty much left alone because the main targets for anglers are either carp or the hordes of silver fish. As a result, with an abundant food source, little angling pressure and being the only predator, and thereby safe from predation other than cannibalism, it is hard to imagine better conditions for such predatory fish to thrive. And thrive they have. Many anglers are now cottoning onto the fact that there are some very big perch in these commercial waters and are therefore reaping the rewards.

When to Go

Having looked at location, I now move to the timing of perch fishing trips, in particular how this is affected by the passing of the seasons. Perch are traditionally considered a fish of the autumn, and certainly this is a very good time to go fishing for them. In common with most species they will feed with a greater frequency as the water begins to cool, trying to lay down fat reserves for the periods when the water is cold which in turn reduces the urge to feed. In autumn, however, the perch are likely to feed throughout the day, particularly if it is one of those where the sky seems to be a blanket of grey, with just the threat of light rain. I consider these to be the absolute optimum in perch conditions and wherever possible I will drop all else to get out on the bank, so long as the weather beforehand is conducive too of course. In reality though there are very few days in the early autumn that will not see the angler with a good chance of success. The only ones that I tend to discard are those increasingly frequent Indian summer-type days despite the fact that on such days the perch are still likely to be feeding at dawn or dusk.

Autumn is a good time for perch fishing: here Mark Barrett has a multiple catch of big perch from the River Lark.

In all probability the reason that perch are particularly associated with the autumn, is just that this season tends to offer the perch angler optimum conditions on a more frequent basis. The water is still relatively mild, the light values are changeable as a result of cloudy, dull days, and increasing rainfall adds a tinge of colour. All this both disguises the angler's tackle and also the perch's presence from its prey. The only autumn days that I consider a real struggle are those when the rivers become strongly coloured and flooded, albeit a seemingly increasing occurrence. Though not complete write-offs, most definitely the perch are restricted in their ability to hunt, and as such tend to rely more on smell than on sight to find their food. Flooded rivers though have the effect of condensing the perch into smaller areas, so in theory if the angler can find these areas, usually the slacker water, then they can still be caught. Moreover, the biggest perch that I ever hooked was lost in such conditions.

I was fishing a near bank slack at extremely close range with the top of my chubber float almost touching the near bank sedges. Suddenly the small livebait was taken and

Cheryl Tomline with a handsome 2 lb 14 oz perch.

the fish went off so powerfully that I was sure I had hooked one of the many nuisance jack pike. As a result, I bullied the fish much harder than I would have done and as the water was very shallow the perch was brought thrashing up onto the surface pretty quickly. Unfortunately, on seeing such an immense perch just a few feet out being unceremoniously hauled in, I made the cardinal mistake of slackening off and unsurprisingly it immediately threw the hook. To this day I cringe at the thought of the loss of that fish through my own stupidity, not least because I am pretty certain that it would have been well in excess of four pounds.

As the season passes into winter the perch activity on the whole slows down. They can still be caught but the periods of time that they feed are much shorter. In my experience, these brief spells of activity tend to be at dusk, and incidentally I have found dawn to be next to useless especially in midwinter. The most likely reason for this is that the water temperature will be at its lowest point and most of the prey fish will be less active than they tend to be at dusk. Winter days can literally boil down to just a half hour's action, around 4 pm as the light fades away, the 'witching hour' as I refer to it. Of course, there will be days when the perch will be active for longer but these tend to be when the water temperature is on the rise, often when a mild south-westerly front has passed through and added a touch of extra water to the rivers and lakes. Again even in these conditions I would expect the bulk of the perch action as the light fades, though the feeding spell could last a bit longer, perhaps even for most of the afternoon especially if the light is poor.

Moving on into the spring, as the water warms the perch turn to spawning. Certainly, as stated, the early part of the spring will offer the perch angler the chance of an outsize specimen as the females become gravid. Even so, this will ultimately lead to a point in the spring where the fishing will completely fade as the fish spawn. When this happens I usually leave them well alone. The fish suffer a great drop in condition at this time of the year, and although in any case they do not feed whilst actually spawning, a female on the point of spawning will be in a very fragile state. I see no reason to inflict potentially serious damage on the fish at this time and tend to veer off and target other species, in all probability right the way through to the following autumn. There are the odd occasions when I will target perch in the late spring and summer months, but in all honesty these tend to be opportunist occasions when, for instance, a perch has appeared within my swim. Nevertheless, I know that for a lot of anglers north of the border in Scotland, perch offer an exciting summer interlude when the pike fishing slows because of the heat. Lures are a particular favourite at this time of the year, as the perch will certainly be in the most aggressive of moods, willing to chase them and hit them with gay abandon. But, as with most predatory fish, they are very prone to problems when returned to the water, usually as a result of being over played and building up lactic acid within their muscle tissues which, incidentally, is a bit like our cramp. This is the main reason I do little in the way of summer perching, and that that I do is confined to early or late in the day, when the water is reasonably cool and the perch most likely to feed.

Tackle

I now want to turn to the tackle needed for perch fishing and, as I hinted at right at the start of this chapter, the perch fisher is rarely one of those who uses the most modern of rigs and/or often tackle. This is because as perch do not grow to huge proportions they can be landed on the most basic of equipment. Despite this comment, to get the best of any form of angling, suitable tackle will make the whole of the proceedings a lot easier and furthermore enjoyable.

Whilst just about any rod will land a perch, certain rods are preferable. Even though they may not be the biggest or hardest fighting of fish, they do offer unique problems when it comes to turning hooked fish into ones on the bank. I would say the main cause of the majority of lost perch is that of hook pulls, and in most cases I credit this to the fish being hooked in the soft membrane around its jaws. Over-strong, unbalanced tackle only further exacerbates this problem and so it is advisable to put a bit of thought into the rod that you use. I use several rods, though only three were bought with the genuine intention of using them for perch. These three are two Drennan super specialist rods in 1.25 lb test curve, and a Fox Avon duo rod with a twin tip section comprising of a 1 lb test curve Avon top and a 0.75 test curve quiver tip section. For most of my perch fishing needs, these three rods will suffice. All are fairly soft-actioned with a through action, which is essential to avoid hooks being ripped from the perch's mouth. The only other rod that I use, other than lure rods, is a 15 to 17 feet commercial carp waggler. I use this for float fishing in very deep water, though admittedly this is a pretty rare occurrence, but it also comes in handy for long trotting on the bank.

When it comes to reels, these are probably one of the least important of items for perching. Any good reel will suffice as long as it offers a good line lay and has spare spools for differing strengths of line. My personal choice is for Shimanos and I tend to use their smaller specimen reels, my favourite being the Stradic model. Apart from this I also use a Young's Purist centre-pin reel, mainly for trotting baits from the boat or bank, and also for fishing at close range. This is simply because it offers far more control whilst playing fish in such situations. On the whole, I fill all these reels with monofilament line of either 4, 6 or 8 lb breaking strain depending upon what method I am fishing at the time. For fishing on a river where the likelihood of hooking anything of any size other than a perch is remote, and when using either lobworms or maggots, I would use 4 lb breaking strain. Where it may be snaggier but where there are no pike I would use the 6 lb for lobworms or livebait. Finally, where pike may be an issue I step up to 8 lb line.

As far as terminal tackle is concerned, essentially we are talking about float fishing, ledgering and lure fishing, so such as floats, ledger weights, shotting patterns, hooks and traces come into the frame. I deal with all this below in the methods section of the chapter.

In addition to the actual fishing tackle referred to, a perch angler will need a seat, electronic bite alarms for ledgering, a landing net, a small unhooking mat and unhooking tools, weighing scales, some means of retention for your catch such as a barbel or pike tube, and a camera. Something to carry your gear and bait, like a small rucksack, is also required as is a quiver or rod holdall.

In passing, a lot of anglers seem to let themselves down as far as the camera and photography is concerned, so I want to comment on this a little here. With the amount of angling writing I do, good photos are a must and the first thing that I consider when buying a camera is just who is likely to be taking the photos. What I mean by this is consider how you fish most of the time. After all, if like me you fish predominantly on your own, then a means of self-take will be essential. With today's modern digital cameras this has been made easy. Having said this, in the moment of catching a really nice fish it is very easy to make very simple mistakes that can completely ruin your shots. My advice is to get your camera gear set up before you start fishing, but at the very least decide where you are going to take any photos should you need to do so. Remember to choose your background very carefully. I have seen many photographs with a cluttered background, or worse still with fences, trees and so on seemingly growing out of the angler's head. Also remember that the choice of background will determine how well your photos turn out. Though a photograph with the river or lake in the background may well seem as if it will look nice, in reality unless you use fill-in flash the most important foreground, and that is you and your catch, will be very dark as the camera will take its lightest reading from off the water and compensates accordingly. A darker more neutral background is a much better bet and that is why you see a lot of photographs with the angler posing in front of a tree, grass or similar. Such foliage is usually a very good bet, plus it has a very handy habit of completely disguising the area where you are fishing.

Baits

So having got our tackle, including photography, sorted out, we come to another key area and that is bait. I said earlier that perch are extremely catholic in their tastes and will pretty much eat anything. Even so, there are the classic baits that are synonymous with the species, and I can think of nothing that fits that label better than the humble worm and in particular the lobworm. There are other natural baits like livebaits and maggots, and then there are the artificial baits or lures.

Natural Bait

Throughout the ages lobworms have always been intrinsically linked with perch fishing and, despite the odd drawback, they still have a major part to play in the modern perch angler's armoury. One is the fact that it is a far from selective bait so they catch just about every perch that swims, from the smallest to the largest. As a result it is not the best bet when you wish to be selective in what you catch. Another drawback is that they are attractive to every other species of fish too. This is not so much of a problem

Perch and worms go hand in hand.

if a nice chub or bream livens up a dull day, but not so great if the same fish goes piling through a producing perch swim.

The many plus points to lobworms outweigh any drawbacks though, not the least of these being the fact that they are extremely easy to procure. A few hours on a damp night at the local sports field will see a supply of lobs that will last many trips. It is a simple thing to creep up on the worms as they lay out of their holes taking in moisture. Tread carefully and quietly, and make sure the torchlight is not shone directly on the worms, otherwise they will shoot straight back down their holes. Once grabbed hold them firmly, but do not immediately try to pull them free as the worm will simply tense in its hole. Just maintain the pressure and eventually the worm will relax its grip and can be completely removed. Incidentally, in hooking a lobworm, I have found the best way is to put the hook point into the worm at the saddle, the band about a third of the way from the pointed end, and then thread the hook into the worm so that the bulk of the shank is covered and the point exposed.

Another thing to remember about worms is that they are extremely high in amino acids, which fish detect to find food. This can be used to great effect by feeding chopped/broken worms into the swim being fished. I also find that worms chopped up with added red maggots are one of the best perch attractors, and if you add a little bit of clouded groundbait to the mix all the better as this will stimulate the small prey fish.

There are other worms that the angler can use in addition to lobworms. All of these will catch perch, but with the exception of the gilt worm I think the rest are really too small to use for the larger fish.

Apart from worms, the best bait of all in my opinion, especially for the bigger perch, are livebaits. Livebaiting itself is a controversial subject for many but my own view is that if you are happy to hook a fish through the mouth then it is somewhat hypocritical to denounce others for putting hooks elsewhere. Moral issues aside, livebaiting is by far the best way to single out the larger perch. Whilst the smaller fish feed on a wide variety of aquatic life, as mentioned earlier the biggest perch will pretty much solely feed on other smaller fish. For the angler wishing to target the bigger perch this fact cannot be ignored and is something to be used to our advantage.

Livebaits should certainly always be caught from the water that the angler is fishing at the time, but this should not be considered as a pain or chore, more so an opportunity as simply by the act of stirring the smaller fish into feeding the perch will be attracted to the swim. Any smaller fish will suffice as a livebait, many of which I mentioned earlier, the only real limit being what can be caught at the venue on the day. My favourite big perch livebaits though are gudgeon and chublets, simply because these are the hardiest of the small fish species. Bleak are also good baits but are the opposite as they will turn up their toes if looked at in the wrong way.

Where the angler is limited by the rules of the fishery, or by their own morals, dead fish are an alternative to live ones, though in my opinion they are far less effective. I have caught perch on deadbaits, but fishing them statically can be very slow. Admittedly, movement can be added to deadbaits by wobbling or sinking and drawing, and this can certainly be an effective way of fishing. But in all reality if I could not use livebaits, I certainly favour worm. By the way, when it comes to sea deadbaits I have found them to be a complete waste of time for perch.

Before leaving the issue of natural baits, there are other baits that will catch perch, probably the main two of those that are used being maggots and prawns. Maggots do play a big part in my perch fishing, though rather more as a loose feed than a hook bait. Nevertheless there are places and occasions where maggots are even better than worms. For example, at one particular commercial fishery I know, a single slow sink-ing red maggot fished within a cloud of falling maggots is the way to catch the big perch, while worms are pretty much ignored. I find this quite amazing and can only put this down to the fact that there are lots of maggots used here so the perch have taken a fancy to them as opposed to worms. Prawns can and do produce the odd big perch, but I tend to shy away from them where carp are present because carp absolutely adore prawns and the perch rarely tend to get much of a look in.

Artificials

Having looked at natural baits it has to be said that one of the most interesting ways of fishing for perch can be with artificial baits or lures. When I was younger many is the time that I would break up a slow day by trying to winkle out a few perch on blade spinners. One of the first places that I ever fished for perch was on a small clay pit near to my home. This water had amazing water clarity and was full of perch that averaged around a pound to a pound and a half. I can vividly recall watching these perch chasing after my spinners into the margins of the lake, fins erect and trying to be the first to nail the Mepps.

These days there are far more lures available to the perch angler than even in my fairly recent youth. Amongst the plugs, spinners and spoons, the perch lure angler is now additionally armed with such as jigs, jelly worms and even flies. I have probably caught more perch on lures in my lifetime than I have pike, mainly because I am a pretty useless lure fisherman, but also because perch can be very accommodating on lures which paper over any angler deficiency.

Artificials/lures are many and varied, and catch a lot of perch.

I have taken a lot of the perch on blade spinners. These lures are still very popular today, and will still catch a lot of perch, but they do tend to attract the smaller perch more readily than the bigger ones. That said though, a few Mepps, or other brand spinners, should always be kept in the lure box for 'scratching' time.

Spoons also have a large part to play for the serious perch angler. Most of my biggest lure caught perch have been caught on spoons with the exception of my personal best lure caught perch, and they really do seem to sort out the biggest perch.

If there is a bigger growth area in lure fishing than jigs, I am pretty unaware of it. Whilst jigs are nothing new, it is only in fairly recent times that British anglers have really come to grips with them as the potent fish catchers that they undoubtedly are. They come in various shapes and sizes, but the principle is similar for all of them in that they are made from soft rubber with a tail of some description at the rear, which will either swirl through the water, or beat through it as movement is imparted into the jig by the angler.

Finally, I come to plugs, nowadays often referred to as crankbaits since the renaissance in lure fishing in the British Isles and the influence of the USA. Whatever term you choose to use, these lures are great perch catchers. They are usually made from plastic or balsa wood. Some float, only diving whilst retrieved, while others will sink and then come up in the water when retrieved. There are also suspending lures that will either rise or fall depending upon the retrieve imparted to them, but will hang in the water at the depth at which they are when the retrieve is ceased.

Methods

I now come to the nitty gritty of perch fishing, namely the methods that are used to catch them. To really know how to get the method right, we need to take into account just exactly how perch feed in any given situation and just as importantly the things that an angler can do that will increase his or her chances of success. To this end I deal with float fishing, lure fishing and ledgering respectively.

Float Fishing

Given what we know about the perch's excellent sight, large mouth and manoeuvrability it would stand to reason that a bait given as much movement as is possible would be the best bet, and certainly I have found this to be so. By and large then, my view is that free roving livebait rigs are definitely a great way to go. And importantly, as with all perch fishing methods, make sure that they are as resistance free as possible. Like their close relation the zander, perch are not tolerant of resistance. Although there are times when this 'rule' goes out of the window, they are few and far between. It is far better to keep your rigs as free running as possible. In a livebait rig, this means using floats that are as small or slim as can be got away with, this also depending upon flow if you are river fishing. My personal favourite floats for perch fishing are the Drennan clear chubber range. These range in size from 1 to 5 swan-shot ratings and should cover any eventuality, but I tend to use the largest 3, 4 and 5 shot rating floats the most as these will easily handle livebaits up to a reasonable size. They also offer another advantage when there is a reasonable flow because you can slightly undershot them and lay on without the float being forced under by the current.

Without a doubt, laying on a livebait is by far my favourite means of fishing for perch, probably because it is the method by which I have caught most of my big fish. The rig that I use is the aforementioned big chubber float, down to a free running Korda running rig. This consists of a very large eyed swivel from which I tie a very short length of 3 lb line and to this are nipped the required number of swan-shot. Below this is a buffer bead large enough to prevent the run ring from passing over the trace swivel. Trace material is a matter of debate within perch angling. Many abhor the use of wire as they feel that this puts the perch off. In the past when the only wire that was available was pike wire, this was almost certainly the case as such wire was very thick

and stiff. However, we are now spoiled for choice as regards the wire that we can use and I strongly believe that where there are pike present, the use of wire is an absolute must.

I use the Drennan super soft green wire in 15 lb breaking strain. I have caught perch on this up to 3 lb 11 oz and never feel that this has put perch off in any way. This wire has the same sort of diameter as 6 to 8 lb line and I do not think there are many perch anglers who would not consider using this as a hook length. It is also extremely pliable and supple and can actually be knotted, though personally I prefer to twist the hook and swivel to it. At the end of the trace, the hooks that I use are either the Drennan super specialist barbel hooks, or ESP stiff rigger hooks. I have used a wide variety in the past and I have come down to these two as they have both proved to be efficient hookers. They do not seem to pull out very easily, and in the case of the barbel hooks they are also a nice matt grey finish which can be useful in very clear water.

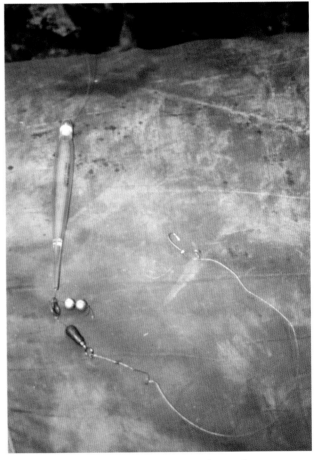

Mark Barrett's standard livebait float rig for perch…

…and a float fished livebait is Mark Barrett's favourite perch method.

For a free roving livebait rig I would still use very similar tactics, however the major difference would be that the free running swivel would be removed and instead the swan-shot would be nipped directly onto the trace, about 3 to 6 inches above the bait, thus making sure that the bait keeps down to the depth required. Any further up the trace and certain fish species such as rudd and bleak will try to swim upwards. Not only does this mean that the bait is not fishing at the required depth, but also that the bait may well end up tangling the rig.

One of the best methods of all to fish livebaits for perch is using a 'CD' rig, a rig already commented on by Steve Ormrod in his eel chapter. It is similar to the pike angler's paternoster rig, but by changing the angle at which the bait sits, and the position of the float within the rig, the rig is completely resistance free, this being an obvious boon for the perch angler.

Moving away from livebaiting, there are times when the angler may wish to use worms as well as such as maggots for bait, and here the use of such a big float may be a hindrance especially on stillwaters. Here perch fishing will require more standard types of float like wagglers. Consequently, for a lot of my perch fishing on commercial type waters where livebait is invariably not allowed I use lobworms fished under a waggler float. On one of the commercials that I fish, the depth drops away in two stages.

151

The first shelf is around 4 to 6 feet deep, from where the water drops away again to a shelf of around 15 to 18 feet before dropping the final time to 25 feet and more. Depending upon the time of year the perch will be in either the first or second shelf. Now with a conventional specimen rod, fishing a waggler at 15 to 18 feet is going to prove problematical if fished in conventional style. Here the use of a sliding waggler becomes necessary.

I use very large, straight peacock wagglers that take a loading of 2 to 4 swan-shot. This is because you will need a bit of weight to pull the line through the eye of the float (or adaptor), without the buoyancy of the float acting unduly as a drag. If the float is too small, what happens is that because of the resistance of the line coming off the spool of the reel, the float and weights will actually start to move back towards the angler as the bait is sinking, and it becomes extremely difficult to position a bait correctly. Of course an easy, albeit expensive, option would be to buy one of the commercial type long float rods. These are very handy tools to have as they allow for easier float fishing in deep water, and in addition the extra length can be a positive boon when trotting on flowing rivers, particularly in conjunction with a centre-pin reel. Most of us have to fish to a budget though, so if you do not wish to splash out on a new rod, then the slider is a good alternative. To set this up, first of all you will need to tie up a sliding stop knot onto the reel line. This can be of power gum or similar, but make sure that whatever you use, it will pass easily through the eyes of your rod and it will stop the float! A lot of modern floats are fitted with adaptors on the base, which incorporates a small swivel. Whilst these are far more free running and easier to use, if your float has this type of fitting then you will have to incorporate a small bead after the knot to act as a buffer for the float. The float is then added of course and set to the depth via plumbing. Your shotting pattern makes a great deal of difference to how the float will work, and indeed signal bites. Because most of these commercial waters incorporate carp in greater numbers than usual I tend to like to get the bait down to the deck fast, and have something to anchor the bait down to the bottom when carp may be moving close by. I also tend to shot my float up, so that one swan is resting on the bottom, about 2 to 3 inches from the hook, whilst the other two (on a three swan float) are about 2 to 3 feet off bottom. This shotting will allow the float to cast and the bait to sink well, whilst the bottom shot will not only anchor the bait, but also in the event of a bite the float will rise in the lift fashion and can result in a fast strike. One final tip with fishing in this manner concerns the positioning of your rod. With the slider, it is essential to have all the line from the tip of the rod to the float sunk, otherwise it will pull the float about a lot. I tend to have the butt at a nice height to strike instantly, either resting on my lap, or on a rest to my right side, and the front rest is set so that the top 6 inches of the rod are submerged.

As the float is cast, the bail arm is left open and line allowed to run out whilst the tip is submerged until the float hits depth. The line is then tightened to the float. The float can actually be tightened down to a point where only the merest tip is showing, but I rarely find this necessary. I have caught some lovely fish like this, and in fact

This 3 lb 8 oz perch was caught by Mark Barrett from a commercial fishery on waggler fished lobworm.

during the writing of this chapter, the perch bug bit quite deeply so a trip to a local commercial was made. As the season had just ended on the rivers, and in some pretty dire weather, I managed to extract a fin perfect 3 lb 8 oz fish on a lobworm and slider.

Lure Fishing

Not surprisingly, another, perhaps somewhat obvious, way of getting movement into the bait is by using artificials/lure fishing. I have already mentioned the main types of lures I use – blade spinners, spoons, jigs and crankbaits/plugs – and initially I again want to stress the necessity of using wire traces if there are pike about. I now turn to some brief comments on how to use these lures.

Spinners are easy to use not least because all you do is cast and retrieve them. My favourite of all of this type of lures is actually a bit of a hybrid spinner, in that it also consists of a plug body, and these are the blue fox lures made by Rapala. I think these are better than a simple bar spinner as when the retrieve is stopped they flutter down to the bottom in a similar way to a sink and draw style bait. This gives the angler the

153

advantage when a slower retrieve is necessary, something that the blade type spinners alone cannot match.

Spoons are a real favourite of mine and have led to lots of success. Perhaps this could be in part due to the size that I use, but for whatever reason a spoon can certainly be the way to outwit the largest perch. I tend to use them around the 6 inch size, and for a very good reason. Some of the biggest perch in England in particular are now in trout reservoirs, these having come to the attention of anglers after being caught during the pike fishing days that are increasingly common. A lot of these perch get caught on spoons and spinnerbaits used by pike anglers. Because trout are also suckers for such types of bait there are usually rules limiting the size of spoons that can be used to 6 inches and above, and yet this is how the perch are usually getting caught. I have had some great days on these reservoirs to the extent that the pike have largely been forgotten because the perch have proved to be so obliging. One such day is worth recounting as it goes to illustrate that small things can really make a great difference to what can be caught.

At Grafham Water the hotspot for just about all species of fish is around the aeration tower. This is a huge attraction for the perch as all structures are, and every morning that the reservoir is open to piking there is a race to get a good spot around the tower. My boat partner Spencer Howard and I had not got off to a great start on the day in question, due in part to some pretty inept bailiffing. My echo sounder had got kicked into the reservoir by another angler, along with other items of kit including the pole to the landing net, not all of which we managed to retrieve. Following this we were late in getting off to the tower so basically had to slot in where we could. We actually finished up a little way off and had a few hours of unsuccessful water thrashing with big rubbers and jerkbaits. The tower became increasingly deserted by the pikers so we managed to move in a bit closer, in fact close enough to be able to work our lures right against the structure. It did not take very long for this move to pay off when Spencer pulled into a fish on a 6 inch silver spoon. This proved to be a very decent perch though exactly how big it was we were never to find out. After I hand landed and unhooked it, I went to pass the fish over to him but in the process it flipped and went straight over the side of the boat. The fact that it was without question a 3 lb plus fish and a new personal best left a very sheepish me I can tell you. Still all was forgotten on the next cast when Spencer pulled into another perch, not quite as big but at 2 lb 14 oz a nice consolation prize. And the action was not to stop there as he again hit into a perch, this one coming adrift before my 'butter fingers' ever got close to it.

Now the interesting thing here was that Spencer and I were basically fishing the same water and with the same pattern of spoon, a Fox gladiator, but whilst he was getting takes on a regular basis, I had yet to have so much as a knock. The only difference between the tackle that we were using was that Spencer was using a silver spoon, whilst mine was copper coloured. Being, I believe, fairly quick on the uptake, I was soon hunting through my lure box for some silver coloured lures. Unfortunately I had no such spoons and the only lure that I could find that had a predominantly

It is not Spencer Howard but another perching partner of Mark Barrett's, Richard Scott, searching out the aeration tower at Grafham Water.

silver colouration was a Fox chubby shad jig in roach pattern. This was soon hurled out alongside the tower and after just a few casts I had a hit on the jig though it quickly came adrift. But only a few casts later a perch finally came to the boat for me, while Spencer had landed a couple more. And a cracker mine was too, weighing in at 3 lb 1 oz. We went on to catch a few more, every single one being caught on silver coloured lures despite trying other colours without success. None was bigger than the first one that I juggled overboard, but it was a very interesting day that taught me an important lesson, namely to keep alternating the lures in case there is, like this particular day, a really strong preference.

Mention has been made of jigs, and it must be said they are probably amongst the most versatile of lures, as unlike others such as spinners or spoons, they can be worked vertically from a boat or, where the bank suits, to keep a jig in the area where the fish are expected to be. With the perch's love of structure this is a huge advantage as effectively the angler can anchor up to, or very close to the structure that holds the perch and work the jig around the structure. Usually they are worked very close to the bottom, just bouncing up and down on the bottom, so that the jig will not only impart movement from its body for attraction, but will also disturb the bottom strata to look like a fish on the feed, or moving around the bottom. The only drawback jig fishing has to offer is that it is a far more difficult facet of lure fishing to get to grips with than say

This 3 lb 1 oz perch was taken by Mark Barrett on a spoon from Grafham Water.

fishing a plug, spoon or spinner. It demands a lot of concentration as the hit can come at any time, yet the angler has to impart just the smallest of movement to really work jigs well. My advice is to put in the effort though as unquestionably perch really love them.

Finally, when it comes to crankbaits/plugs although they are easily and simply fished on a cast and retrieve basis, their variations – floating, sinking, suspending – means they do take some getting used to. Plus there is the fact that there are thousands of patterns. The best advice I can give is to choose a plug that suites the type of water you are fishing, and to do this simply use trial and error until success is found.

Ledgering

There will be times when for varying reasons of either casting distance, weather or flow float fishing may prove to be not the optimum presentation. In this instance the angler will need to ledger to get the best results. Now I have to say here and now that ledgering is pretty much a last resort for me. It does undoubtedly catch fish, and I have taken some large perch ledgering for them, but wherever conditions suit I find that float fishing will outscore. However, there are times when the use of a float is unsuitable and here the angler will need to adapt accordingly. Ledgering itself can be as simple or as complicated as the angler deems to make it. My view though, and it is the same for whatever species I am fishing for, is to keep rigs as simple as possible. For perch, probably the most straightforward rig of all is a simple link ledger. In my case this comprises similar components to the chubber float rig, but minus the float of course. This gives a nice, simple, free running rig that offers the minimum of resistance to a taking perch. Depending upon the distance and flow rate, weight can be added or subtracted easily by either adding swan-shot, or if extra distance is required then I use either a flattened pear lead, or an arsley-type bomb, or if a swimfeeder is required then I use an oval blockend type of swimfeeder for maggots or a cage feeder for crumb. At the rod end indication is either provided by a quivertip if roaming a river, or a bite alarm and bobbin if more than one rod or livebaits are being used. Very soft quivertips are a must and for perch I use my Fox Avon duo rod with the .75 lb test curve quiver top section, but it also has a choice of interchangeable quiver tops. In my opinion, a rod of this type is a must, as it gives the angler more flexibility as the choice of quiver is used to match the conditions on the day. With my bobbin rig I use the Delkim alarms as they are extremely sensitive, and a set of lightweight hanger bobbins that are attached to the fitting via a cord. These are a good option, as adding swan-shot to the cord beneath the bobbin can change the weighting of the bobbin very easily. Beware though, particularly when using livebaits, as a feather light bobbin can result in a few problems; the action of the bait itself will cause the bobbin to rise and fall slightly which can drive both the angler and any others close by mad.

So having looked at perch and perch fishing based on my experience mainly in the east of England it seems opportune to look at a contrasting aspect of perching, namely fishing for canal perch in the north-west of England.

Canal Perch

Big perch from canals are a very different proposition to big perch from any other water. As I said, to catch big perch from a river, you have to find such as the slower/deeper water or a snag as the perch will invariably be close by. Big perch on stillwaters, especially in winter, will be in the deepest area of the pond, lake or reservoir. It is then a matter of selecting such as the right conditions, bait presentation, time of day and so on. Canals though are different in that there can be literally miles of featureless water so you are often left wondering where to start your search for big perch. Brian Steele has been fishing for these canal perch for many years in north-west England, and here he relates some of his experiences.

As with any species, location is the key to success; if you find the fish you are in with a chance of catching them. It would be reasonable to assume that, for example, a moored boat or barge would be a great place to start the search for big perch or maybe that willow hanging in the water. These sorts of places scream big perch but often it is not that straightforward at all. Big canal perch are in fact never far away from shoals of food fish. Being stalkers by nature, they like to creep up on unsuspecting prey, get as close as possible and then engulf them in a split second. They often do not want to waste valuable energy chasing prey, and after they have fed they then lie on the bottom motionless. They can stay switched off for days or even weeks after feeding. Taking these factors into account, big perch are a difficult species to target on canals. They are never far away from a food source, they feed for short periods of time, and they spend long periods of time switched off.

So how can you target big perch on canals so that you have a reasonable chance of success? You could spend all your spare time on the canal with a variety of baits, including livebaits, and lures, covering many miles of the towpath and in so doing you may even catch one… eventually, of course. Or you can catch one more methodically, by design if you will, and this is likely to be a far better and more successful way. And for me by far the most exciting method in angling is stalking. Yes, it is possible to stalk big perch on canals, this being something I have done many times. To actually see a big perch in the water is exciting enough but to see one at close quarters and watch it engulf your bait; it certainly does not get any better than that.

At the outset it has to be said that as far as canals are concerned, in summer they are pretty much a waste of time for big perch; there is simply too much boat traffic and there are also lots of food items available for the perch. Late autumn into winter is the time to be on the canal for the big 'sergeants'. You need to find a stretch that has prolific weed growth in the summer months together with deeper water. The weed will keep suspended sediment to a minimum and this, together with the lack of boat activity and the drop in water temperature, means that such stretches of canal will invariably be crystal clear in winter.

Once you have found yourself such a stretch, you have done the hard part but you must then return, preferably after there have been a few frosts. If possible pick a bright, sunny day with no wind and take a pair of polarised sunglasses and a peaked cap. The aim is to search the canal bed for signs of a big perch being present. Walk slowly and be fully focused on the task in hand, searching every inch of the canal bed. Do not write off a stretch of canal because it 'does not look right'. Be cautious, control your footfall to cause the absolute minimum disturbance and you are likely to see lots of other species as well as perch. Once you find a big perch mark the area with something that cannot be easily disturbed or moved and then carry on as there will be more.

Having located perch holding areas it is time to catch them. All you need for bait is a big fat lobworm while the tackle needs to be similar to that required for catching small carp. A rod with a test curve of 1.4 lb and a decent reel loaded with a good quality monofilament line of around 4 lb breaking strain is ideal, coupled with a very sharp size 6 or 8 hook.

This 3 lb 4 oz canal perch took Brian Steele's lobworm.

Brian Steele with a brace of specimen perch: 3lb and 2 lb 7 oz caught on a dead roach and lobworm respectively from the Bridgewater Canal.

Set your rod up before you commence your search and although the perch may not be exactly where they were located before, they will be close by. I like fishing freeline style, so there is no need for a float or weights. The worm will act as your casting weight although to be honest, an underarm swing is generally enough. Once you see a perch, keep as low as possible ensuring you are not seen and that your shadow is not cast across the fish. If possible position yourself behind the fish. Hook on a big lobworm and nip the tail off; I usually hook them once through the saddle. Swing the bait out and let it 'plop' on the water, ideally so it settles twelve to eighteen inches in front of the perch. Once the worm hits the bottom let the line go slack and the perch will lift off the bottom slightly, moving towards the worm

159

very slowly, until it is two or three inches away. It will then tilt up, the gills will flare and the worm itself will disappear. Strike immediately this has happened, thus ensuring your fish will not be deep hooked, and keep a tight line as any slackness during the fight could result in a lost fish. Do not be too disappointed with the fight and do not expect any long surging runs; the fight is more of a head shaking defiance but it sometimes brings success to the perch so be aware. Once you have landed the fish take great care with the unhooking and photographing process, remembering, for example, to use an unhooking mat as big perch do not cope well with rough handling. Also keep the fish out of the water for the absolute minimum time possible, and when returning it try to lower the fish into the water by hand, allowing it to slip into the canal once it is fully recovered. If this is not possible due to the height of the banking or it is too dangerous, lower the fish into the water in your landing net.

Remember that big perch are a very worthy quarry. Their striking beauty and bristling defiance makes them one of our most impressive freshwater fish. That specimen caught by stalking will surely remain in your memory for a very long time.

The reader will surely agree that Brian's piece conveys the very essence of perch and perch fishing.

A Memorable Perch

Before drawing this chapter to a close, I now have but one unforgettable tale to relate of how, when everything comes right, I tangled with a big perch.

It was on a mild November day a few years ago that I landed my most memorable perch. The day itself was still reasonably warm, but best of all there was a pall of grey cloud that blotted out the entire sky overhead, with just the occasional shower, or light drizzle to contend with. If you could have written a better day to be perch fishing, then one would be accused of lying! My chosen venue for the day was a small river where I have spent a lot of time in recent years perch fishing, namely the River Lark in Cambridgeshire. The Lark is a really lovely river in places, and my chosen area for the day was one such place, full of overhanging trees and just as importantly as far as perch were concerned, man made boat jetties and moored boats. The river itself was in very fine fettle with just a hint of colour and probably a couple of inches of extra water in from the summer levels. All in all it looked like a great day to be perching, but only time would ultimately decide.

I was joined for the day by my one of my best friends of many years' standing, Richard Scott, and because of this we both set up fairly close to allow us to chat pretty easily. With this in mind it was somewhat strange that for most of the morning Richard really struggled to get a bite, only the odd small perch and jack pike grabbing his livebaits or worms. On the other hand, I had had a great start to the day with a number of fish between 1 lb 8 oz and 2 lb 8 oz, plus a lot of smaller fish on the worm. Eventually Richard could take it no longer and moved to the left of my position, and soon accounted for some nice perch, before hooking into something in a whole different league. Our suspicions were soon confirmed when a large pike rolled in the swim before once again tearing off downstream.

With only an Avon rod and 6 lb line the fight was long and protracted and in reality probably did his perch swim not a lot of good, but eventually I managed to shoehorn a 17 lb 12 oz pike into the net. Richard was understandably delighted with what was a stunning example of a pike, and was busy relating the tales of derring-do to another friend, Russell Brennan, on the phone when my float sailed away again. Upon striking I remarked to Richard that I thought it was another 2 lb plus fish, to which he replied 'do you want a hand with the net?' Initially I declined his offer and he went back to his phone call but very quickly afterwards the fish rolled on the surface and I could see that this perch was an absolute monster. I immediately turned to Richard and said something like 'put that phone down and grab the net!' Richard quickly did as he was told and thankfully made no mistake with the netting. As a result there soon lay in the

Mark Barrett and a magnificent 3 lb 11 oz perch which took a float fished livebait.

folds of the net a truly massive perch, not only as far as this river was concerned but also for any other. After a few seconds of stunned silence we put the fish onto the scales for a weight of 3 lb 11 oz; it was a really fat lady perch and one that I was completely in awe of, from the start of the capture to its release. After the photos had been taken we both returned to our perching. Though the rest of the day passed me by without much action, Richard went on to take a perch just shy of 3 lb. It was truly a great day of perch fishing.

Conclusion

I have caught plenty of big perch since the aforementioned fish, but to this day that capture remains the most memorable one, simply because it was the first true giant that I had caught. Furthermore, it was from a river where the thought of such a fish would have been passed over as a pure fisherman's tale. Yet therein lies the true beauty of perch fishing, for there are no named fish and the stocking level can only ever be guessed at. The perch is truly one of the last wild fish, a fish that has brought me many hours, days and even weeks of enjoyment. Surely you cannot beat that great moment as the float sails away and you strike in earnest. You never know if it will be another juvenile delinquent, or 'the biggest of all the fish'. Enjoy!

6
Zander

Neville Fickling

A n awful amount of water has flowed, literally it has to be said, under the bridge since the introduction of the zander to British waters. They are a non-native species introduced lawfully but then spread by a combination of natural movement and illegal introductions. For good or bad they are here to stay and most sensible anglers seem to accept this. A few have even decided to devote their fishing lives to catching them. For myself, I am in the in-between position because I enjoy fishing for zander but I have other fishing interests as well. As a result I have had an on-off relationship with the species but despite this I fished for them intensively between 1968 and 1995 (this explains the fact that some of the photos in this chapter might seem a little dated, though no less relevant I might add!). That is a lot of fishing experience and I am going to add to it in the years ahead. To this end it should be remembered that zander have been present in the River Trent for about twenty years and, with only the odd exceptions, no-one has really got to grips with catching them. I have had a few zander from the Trent so far, but hope to get more and a much better understanding of them in the future.

Where then did the British zander come from? Well it all started prior to 1878 when several attempts were made to introduce zander to England. A man called Nielsky and a group of other fishermen took sixty hours to transport two dozen zander through gales and then thick fog to London, from where they were taken by rail and finally horse and carriage to Woburn. Here twenty-three fish of about 2 lb each were placed into two lakes there. Further introductions followed, but the plot does not thicken until 1950 when thirty, 5 inch fish from Woburn were stocked into the main lake at Claydon, Buckinghamshire. A more unsuitable venue could hardly be imagined, but despite this they survived. Then in 1960 Swedish zander were stocked into a pit at Mepal in Cambridgeshire. These zander have been there ever since, though with little heard of them.

In 1963 the story really starts with Woburn zander transferred to stock ponds at Hengrave Hall near Bury St Edmunds. On 18 March a hundred zander were then moved from Hengrave to the Relief Channel of which ninety-seven survived. They went on to thrive and by 1968 they had reached double figures in size and were already spreading to other waterways connected to the Relief Channel. After the colonisation of the Great Ouse system the spread of zander was mainly by devious and naughty means. While it is true that the Suffolk Stour and Abberton Reservoir received their zander via a pipeline, as did Grafham Water, almost all other occurrences of zander have been by illegal or at best dubious means. I remember seeing Coventry anglers keep-netting zander in 1974. And what happened then? Yes, a few years later they appeared in the Coventry and Oxford Canal. Was it a coincidence? Possibly, I guess. A friend of mine then misguidedly stocked fourteen zander into Coombe Abbey Lake. They then appeared in the River Severn after 1980 and they continued to move and spread around ending up in the Gloucester Canal, River Thames, River Nene, River Trent, Warwickshire Avon and countless stillwaters. Recently one turned up in the River Yare. It has to be pointed out that the movement of zander to waters which would not otherwise be colonised by them is purely down to the actions of selfish individuals. It must be nice to sit there thinking that you might have negatively affected a really good pike fishery by introducing such competitors; any area of water will only support a certain biomass of predators according to the numbers of prey fish. Do not get me wrong because I do like zander, of course. After all, who cannot be captivated by striking into a nice fish which bends the rod into an arc, then repeatedly swirls on the surface before plunging to the bottom and eventually coming to the net. But I would really hope that some of our surviving good pike fishing is going to be kept as just that. By adding another major predator, zander, to pike waters it surely goes without saying that you are asking for trouble.

Where zander fishing started for Neville Fickling back in 1968: the Polver Drain outfall on the Relief Channel.

The last thing a roach ever sees – the large mouth, jaws and teeth of a zander.

The situation now is such that if you want to catch a zander you can do so in much of the southern half of England. I doubt though if one single zander angler can tell you how to tackle more than half a dozen of the waters they now inhabit; the geographical spread is now just too great. Fortunately the basic principles involved in catching them are similar wherever you go.

There are a number of things then that I intend to do in this chapter. First, I briefly look at the zander's biology and behaviour before providing pointers as to the most favourable water conditions for catching them. Thereafter, I look at their location; this after all, and as always in all fishing, is often the real key to actually catching them. I then discuss tackle followed by bait and then guide the reader through the most important methods used to catch them. Some memorable zander fishing sessions are discussed before I finish with a basic guide to the main zander waters, along with a discussion of what is a good zander and the new zander record.

Biology and Behaviour

It may surprise some to know that actually there are several varieties of zander in Europe where it is known by other names such as 'sander', 'sandel', 'gos' and 'snockbaar'. The actual varieties include *Lucioperca volgenis* found mainly in Austria and South Russia, particularly the River Volga, and *Lucioperca sandra* found in the Danube, North

165

Russia, Scandinavia, Hungary and North Germany. Meanwhile, in North America we have the walleye, *Stizostedion vitreum*.

Then there is our zander, *Sander lucioperca/Stizostedion lucioperca*, which like the other varieties, resembles a cross between pike and perch resulting in them sometimes being called pikeperch. However, it is not a relation or member of the pike family, and not a hybrid of the two, though it is a member of the perch family. They originated in Eastern Europe, Russia and southern Siberia but have spread to western Europe occurring from southern Scandinavia down to northern Italy and Spain. They are like the perch in many ways with, for example, two handsome dorsal fins, the first and spiny one being erected when it is about to attack prey. The fins on the lower part of the body are broad and well formed. They are more streamlined than perch though, a little like pike. They have large eyes and are generally a green-brown in colour with darker vertical bars on their sides. Their notoriously predatory nature is indicated by the large, heavily toothed mouth. Remember though that, like all predators, they only kill to eat and, despite what some might say, they do not, for example, swim round in packs killing whole shoals of fish for fun.

Populations of zander can increase quickly but generally they have a limited home range. Not surprisingly perhaps, their impact on recipient fisheries depends on the rate of expansion of the zander population and the ability of resident prey fish to withstand an additional predator.

Zander spawn from spring to early summer in shallower water. Their pale yellow eggs, which stick to plants and stones, are guarded by both parents until they hatch five to ten days later. The young fish eat water fleas and plankton before moving on to fish fry and small fish more generally. Larger fish often patrol open water as solitary individuals while the smaller ones are quite sociable and like to shoal up and stay in more limited areas. They like the deep, calm waters of both rivers and stillwaters with their actual habitat varying according to the season, for instance, over pebbles where possible until the winter when they retreat to pits and trenches. Wherever they are, as we will see, the water tends to be turbid, that is cloudy and muddy, for much of the time.

Water Conditions

Having mentioned water, I now want to look at the types of water and conditions where we will find zander. Starting with rivers the general rule is that shallow clear rivers rarely if ever support a zander population. The same applies with shallow clear and weedy lakes. By shallow I mean an average depth of 6 feet. We can also safely suggest that drains that average 6 feet in depth and which are clear are not the best place to find zander. However, as soon as you add coloured water into the equation the situation changes dramatically. Zander will thrive in 3 feet of very coloured water; I know because I have had fish to 15 lb 15 oz out of coloured water which was that shallow. Why is this then? Well the zander's eyes are adapted for seeing in conditions

A personal best 15 lb 15 oz zander for Neville Fickling from the Old Bedford; it was taken in shallow, coloured water.

of low light. A special layer reflects light that would have bounced back out of the eye back onto the retina. Much more efficient use of the available light is therefore made and this gives the zander an advantage over less well adapted predators such as pike. Of course, where there is plenty of light the zander is at a disadvantage simply because it does not have eyelids or an iris. In particular, I suspect that zander are uncomfortable in bright sunshine in shallow water.

You would think the answer to the shallow clear water problem would be to seek cover and then hunt at night. Well there are a handful of drains where the zander do just this and the nocturnal sport can be quiet good with some surprisingly good fish caught as a result. On some of our big rivers such as the Trent zander have not become the dominant predator. Again I presume that is because the water is not deep and fairly clear. On the other hand if we look at the Severn, where the mid and tidal reaches are much deeper than on the Trent, zander do thrive.

167

Another important question to address is when to fish for them. We still have a close season on our rivers and drains and long may that continue. Our predatory fish are at their easiest to catch in the spring and I honestly feel that they are under enough pressure at the moment without the addition of all round the year fishing. A lot of stillwaters are of course open all season and I do not have a problem with this because it is quite possible for the fishery owner or club to impose restrictions as to when fishing is carried out. On rivers and drains particularly where many clubs are involved it would be almost impossible to have a coherent close season policy. Club 'A' on one side of the river could have a close season while club 'B' on the other side might not. The whole idea of a close season will then be negated. Unfortunately the National Federation of Anglers in particular are pushing for the abolition of the rivers' close season and I this is something I am totally against.

For most of us then 16 June to 14 March is the time slot allocated to us to fish for zander. In fact, you can catch zander very successfully from 16 June as they will not have finished spawning that long and they can be really feeding with a vengeance. However, as you get into July and August things tend to slow down. There is also a big problem with weed these days. Floating weed, in particular duckweed and 'cot' can drive you nuts. As a result, at the present if I was fishing the Fens I would start in September. On

A frosty dawn on the Middle Level; in conditions like this the zander tend to be nocturnal.

Neville Fickling with a fine 11 lb zander from the Middle Level.

the Trent though, where weed is not a problem, summer zander fishing is viable though the nights tend to be rather short and the days impossibly long. The magic months for zander used to be September and October particularly on the Fens. Unfortunately the warmer weather means that it is still like fishing in the summer. Fishing in the early autumn can involve both daytime and nocturnal sessions. It has never ceased to amaze me how zander can switch between feeding in the middle of the day to the middle of the night. I am sure there are exceptions, but I have found that the hungrier zander are the more likely they are to feed in the middle of the day, while really well fed zander tend to be more nocturnal.

Once we get into the winter proper then water conditions tend to play a big part as far as the actual fishing is concerned. Cold, clear water conditions are usually a waste of time in the depths of winter. They can be caught at night though and I have referred to this in the memorable zander fishing section below. Coloured water changes everything with a much better chance of daylight activity. As a rule it seems the lower the water temperature is, the less zander activity there will be. They still feed when it is really cold, but it takes a long time to digest a meal so intervals between feeding tend

169

to be extended. If I was asked for ideal winter conditions I would choose two or three days after peak water levels matched with air temperatures of 12° to 14°C. This sets the water temperature rising and zander do respond well in this situation. Coloured water also sees the bigger zander hunting, perhaps more regularly than the smaller ones. I have certainly seen few small ones in these floodwater conditions. Although you will catch zander during the day when the water is coloured you will, of course, catch fish during the night as well. Generally though they tend to feed somewhat erratically in coloured water and overall you certainly cannot rule out any time of day. For years the end of February or the last two weeks of the fishing season were red hot zander fishing times. Unfortunately we now keep getting cold spells at the 'wrong' time of the year so it pays to be flexible and take your chances when they present themselves.

Location

Location of zander in the variety of waters they inhabit is naturally increasingly difficult the bigger the water is. They seldom show themselves and you are unlikely to see one roll on the surface or strike at prey. Even if you stood and watched the water for a week you would probably not see a single sign of a zander. It can happen and does of course, but it is so rare as to generally be a complete waste of time. All zander location then has to be done by trial and error, with perhaps the odd bit of observation helping.

If, for example, I had to start from scratch on really big water such as the Relief Channel, the first thing I would do is to try and find where the food fish are. A long walk at first light or dusk should reveal the answer. Grebes and cormorants are only good pointers if the food fish are really concentrated. If you walk two miles and see grebes every four hundred yards that is not a lot of use, though if they are all concentrated in one area then that is different.

When you have had years fishing a water such as the Channel you will know where the favourite spots are regardless of the food fish. Unfortunately most newcomers to waters such as the Channel lack that knowledge and have to do things the hard way. Even so, knowing too much can be a disadvantage because as time moves on, hot swims change and my big problem when I fish a water I know really well is that I tend to keep going back to spots that have been very consistent in the past. Recently that has not worked so starting from scratch is not all bad news. Ignoring my bad experiences, what follows seems to work for most people.

There are two basic modes of zander location and these are much the same as you would employ while pike fishing. Simply put, they are picking a known spot and sitting and waiting, or moving around trying to find fish. Sitting in a known spot has certainly worked for plenty of people over the years. It may be slow work, but if you have two or three days to fish, the end result is probably worth the wait. A lot of people enjoy 'session fishing' where you sit it out in a known swim and wait for the zander to come to you. There is nothing wrong with this, and after all fishing surely is supposed to be enjoyment and not hard work.

170

The alternative is to move around searching out the water. This is not a 'better' method, but it is an option for those with itchy feet who struggle to sit still for three days. Years ago I found that there were often groups of zander scattered along a drain which though willing to feed had to be found first. They were not actively hunting, but shoaled up in areas which defied any means of pinpointing them other than moving around until they were found. The oft mentioned leap-frogging or rod-hopping is the method here and this simply involves moving a rod along the bank every, say, thirty minutes. If you fish four rods then each rod gets two hours in a spot. This might be a bit slow for some and can be accelerated to every fifteen minutes if you want to cover more water. Environment Agency rules prohibit spreading rods over great distances, but you can have baits spread by simply walking thirty yards up or downstream casting and bring the rods back to where you are fishing. From one swim you can have a spread of sixty yards with baits at sixty to eighty yards and twenty to thirty yards across, thus covering the full width of waters a hundred yards wide like the Channel.

Before anyone suggests that a spread of baits like that suggested is not required I would like to mention a day years ago when a friend of mine fishing opposite me blanked on the Channel while I had nineteen zander on my side. They were simply not

The rods are in on the Relief Channel; note the size of the water.

Another large, at times daunting water, the Middle Level Drain.

on his side of the drain, yet with braid and good casting, and if you do not have a mate opposite you, the far side of the drain can be reached. The mobile method keeps you interested, though when it gets dark you should hopefully have picked a decent spot for the night. Like many others, I am not up to moving around in the night.

Interestingly bridges are still popular areas to fish for zander. Though I can think of some pretty good spots within five hundred yards of some bridges, generally bridges are sit and wait areas. They also offer the advantage of a short walk to the car. If there are food fish around a bridge then you are obviously in with a better chance than if there is nothing edible in the area.

Those readers who have boned up on zander fishing by reading some of the more popular magazines and weeklies might be forgiven for thinking that all zander are highly conscious of resistance and this must be avoided at all costs. Now while there are situations where this is the case, there are also plenty where resistance is the last thing you worry about. It is very much a 'horses for courses' situation. Zander in some waters would pull your rod in rather than let go of the bait. On other waters dropped runs are the norm. It might be a dangerous generalisation, but in my experience most dropped runs are from small zander. They can be absolute buggers on livebaits because they will often try to tackle baits they are destined to struggle to eat. Just like any other predator a free offering is likely to be attacked while it is still alive even if it is too big to take. This is certainly what causes most dropped runs from zander when livebaiting. Dropped runs are also a feature of deadbaiting. To understand this you have to juggle a few ideas in your head. For a start zander are scavengers, but the smaller younger fish are less interested in picking up dead fish. Even so, they will have a look, but because the prey is offering little in the way of stimulation, that is by trying to get away, they soon get bored (yes I know zander do not get bored like us, but the end result is the same). Very well fed zander can also be finicky just like well fed pike. They are so well fed that they can be tempted to feed, but generally unless the prey struggles and provides some stimuli they can drop the bait. And for that matter, a well fed zander can be 10 oz or 10 lb.

Generally trying to reduce resistance is a waste of time unless you want to catch tiny zander. In fact, if I may be so bold, the situation we see with zander fishing may be like that we saw with carp fishing in the seventies. In those days carp anglers went to great trouble to reduce resistance and to hit 'twitchers'. When someone discovered that a fixed lead and exposed hook produced a storming run, the twitcher hitting was condemned to the dustbin of carp fishing history.

Little zander are frequently the cause of dropped runs.

Tackle

Turning to tackle, when I am fishing for zander I am after fish over 3 lb and my tackle is simply at the lighter end of the gear I use for pike fishing. I use size 6 trebles, 28 lb wire and a minimum of 30 lb braid. Rods are my 3 lb test Dictators and reels a variety of Daiwa free spool reels though the free spool feature is only ever used in running water. For those fishing waters where there are lots of small zander you might well decide to scale down and this is acceptable, however please do not scale down to silly levels. Even though it is unlikely, if you hook an upper double figure pike in summer on 10 lb line you are going to exercise it to death. My bite indication is pretty conventional, with Delkims as the bite alarm matched with Fox drop-off bobbins. The advantage with the Delkims is that you get the odd bleep when zander are being naughty, that is they pick the bait up and just sit there with it. This does not happen very often, but one afternoon and night it happened several times and I simply struck once the alarm had bleeped a couple of times. I landed quite a few zander in that session, but have to admit it has not happened since.

My end tackle is about as simple as can be, a simple running ledger for deadbaits and ledgered lives and a sunken float paternoster for livebaits. I tend to have my drop-off bobbins set so that I do not get false alarms. It never ceases to amaze me how many anglers suffer endless false alarms because they do not set the clips on their bobbins tight enough.

So, having had a quick look at tackle, I now turn to bait and methods.

Bait and Methods

As I said the two main methods I use are ledgering and paternostering, but bait choice for zander is the cause of some debate as unsurprisingly, as with many things angling, opinions do differ. When I was catching zander quite merrily in the 1970s and 1980s, a 3 inch slimy covered eel section was the top bait. It could be cast as far as you like, would stay on for a couple of fish and went some way to deter the small eels that sometimes drove you batty (though admittedly these days many of us would love to see more of these bootlaces). Small natural deads such as roach naturally caught plenty of zander, but if I could get them, small dace and chub seemed to work better. These days lamprey and smelt will also catch zander. Far more interesting is the fact that plenty of zander anglers nowadays have picked up good zander on what are considered to be baits which are a waste of time. I refer to oily sea baits such as herrings, mackerel and sardines. It is thirty-nine years since I caught my first zander and I have only managed to catch one zander on a sea bait proper. That fish was a six pounder in March of 1971 and this particular herring was injected with cucumber juice because I was desperately trying to fool the pike into thinking the herring was not a herring. I have soaked an awful lot of sea baits over the years and zander have been singularly absent in my catches. I should say though that a lot of my deadbaiting was done in daylight in clear water conditions with low water temperatures and, bearing in mind what I wrote earlier, we know these conditions are hardly ideal for catching zander. Of course, plenty of pike were caught which is hardly surprising because I was pike fishing after all. Despite my record, readers should keep an open mind and a sardine, herring or small mackerel on one rod might well prove to be a selective bait. I have done this but would not fish such baits on all rods because on some waters you would probably simply die of boredom.

Deadbaits catch a lot of zander, but I am never one to put all my eggs in one basket. Even when I am getting all my zander on deadbaits I will try to fish one rod with a livebait. After all if we are allowed to fish up to four rods it seems a little insane to fish all of them with deads. I have experienced plenty of situations where livebaits have been a waste of time, but equally there have been times when a livebait has produced a very big fish. After October, fishing at night with livebaits has come up trumps many times, even in situations which make livebait presentation difficult. I remember getting a thirteen pounder from the Old Bedford in November in only three feet of water. I had to use a very short paternoster link to keep the bait from tangling with the reel line. That fish was the biggest of the session and the fact that the next double also fell to a livebait convinced me that the slog of carrying buckets of bait, which I had caught earlier I might add, along the bank was certainly well worth the effort.

I fish my livebaits on a sunken paternoster rig coupled with the usual drop-off bobbin and Delkim alarm. I also adapt my ledgered deadbait rig to a ledgered livebait when I am convinced that livebaits are the best bet. Baits are mounted head down with the bait on the bottom or sometimes a piece of polystyrene attached to the trebles to keep it working off the bottom. I do not often use big livebaits, though I have had zander to 8 lb on 8 oz roach baits, because all the evidence is that zander prefer small baits and that evidence in my case includes a two year MSc degree which among other things studied the diet of the zander. I know they will take big baits, but I suspect that they will take a small bait just as, or even more, readily.

Lures

Lures are an interesting option mainly because as far as zander are concerned there is still a lot to learn about the approach. I have had a few fish to 7 lb on lures and have deliberately lure fished for zander on many occasions, but not with notable success. What I have learned is probably not the same as those who have fished for zander more extensively with lures. Most of my lure-caught zander have come by fishing slowly and deeply with spoons such as Tobies and bar spoons. Odd ones have fallen to small deep diving plugs and one even took a 6 inch replicant in the dark. Other anglers have had fish to 12 lb trolling deep invaders in the Fens. That excellent and ever enthusiastic angler, Mick Brown, has had a lot of zander on all sorts of lures. He is particularly keen on vertical jigging with small soft lures. At the moment I have not had a chance to do this because the waters I fish are too shallow.

Neville Fickling returns an 8 lb walleye taken on a leech baited jig in Canada.

I have though caught walleye in Canada using worm or leech-baited rigs which are bounced up and down on the bottom. They certainly catch a stack of fish doing this and sooner or later we are going to have to try it. It is rather like fishing a baited spinnerbait up and down. I am not sure that walleye and zander behave exactly the same; walleye may be more inclined to feed on invertebrates than zander which is why the American and Canadian techniques work so well for them.

It is important to stress that once you have caught your zander, whether it was on a lure, deadbait or livebait, you need to get them back alive. Zander are fairly frail fish and when water temperatures are high they can easily be over exercised if you do not land them quickly. Similar comments apply to unhooking, weighing and photographing them; speed is the essence. A period of rest in a pike tube is usually the option if a zander is struggling to swim off. As the water temperature falls, problems with zander generally decrease. Though I have sacked zander in the past it is not really a good idea as their teeth get caught in the sacking material. The landing net is probably the best option for a short rest before a photograph. I use a couple of bank sticks to hold the arms above water level. Whereas a pike or carp might be naughty and jump out of a net set up like this, zander are very well behaved and usually sink to the bottom. There is always a risk to the fish when fishing for zander, but look at it this way: I have had only a couple die over the years, plus a few badly hooked ones which I took home to eat. These were only small fish and years ago I admit I quite enjoyed eating them. These days, however, laziness and the desire not to cut fish up in the kitchen has seen me buy haddock instead. That is not to say that it is immoral to take a damaged fish to eat. You can hardly justify using livebaits if you are going to veto the eating of the odd small zander. Bear in mind though that clonking a ten pounder on the head will probably get you lynched if others find out.

So having hopefully provided some helpful tips on fishing for zander, I now turn to describing some unforgettable zander sessions.

Steve Croll quickly weighs and returns a double figure zander to the water so ensuring minimum stress to the fish.

177

Memorable Zander Sessions

At the outset I have to admit that, like many others, I have had an awful number of dismal zander fishing sessions as well. Yes, I know you are supposed to enjoy the blanks as well as the good trips and I am sure I did at the time. Unfortunately coinciding with the passage of time, the memory of the poor trips usually weighs heavily when I think about them now. Hopefully to inspire the reader, I am going to relate some of the better sessions here. As I do so I will try to show how certain weather and water conditions can contribute to an exceptional catch. It is also worth emphasising, however, that a long term campaign can often produce the results you desire.

It is September 1974 and we were experiencing a rare southerly gale. It was blowing directly down the Relief Channel and had churned the normally clear waters into a muddy ribbon of water. Pike fishing was out of the question, but experience in 1968, in summer flood conditions, suggested that conditions were ideal for zander. My then fishing companion Andrew Mack and I opted to fish the Channel downstream of Stowbridge. The spot we favoured was peg 13; incidentally in those days almost all of the Channel was permanently pegged. We were on the west bank, but because the wind was straight down the river the high flood bank provided very little cover.

I have no idea how strong the wind was in actual Beaufort scale figures, but it must have been force ten or eleven. We could hardly stand up and erecting an umbrella was totally out of the question. We opted to huddle down behind the odd straggly bush and rods were angled into the wind. We probably had to use the elastic band over the top of the rest trick to keep the rods in place. Bite indicators of any sort were a waste of time though in those days it was at least a year before any of us got our hands on the first decent head type indicators, the Optonic. We had to opt for slackening the clutch off and a piece of silver paper in front of the reel on the line gave a visual indication of a run.

We only had two runs that day, one was a 12 lb 9 oz zander to me which was a big fish in those days and Andy had a 19 lb pike with both coming on legered roach and rudd deadbaits respectively. Both fish gave confident runs against the clutch before we opened the bale arm. The water was as coloured as you could get short of being solid. It was a classic case of a big zander being active in diabolical conditions, though what the pike was doing feeding as well is anyone's guess.

Let me now jump forward to 1978 and I was fishing on the Middle Level above Three Holes Bridge. I had dropped onto an interesting spot a while ago, even though I had always thought the junction between the Middle Level and Pophams Eau was the place to fish. To this day I am amazed that I had enough bait to last the session which was to consist of a morning with twenty-five zander to 9 lb coming to my net. I suspect I was cutting baits up and recovering baits shed by the fish as I was playing them in. The drain where I was fishing was only about 30 yards wide, but it seemed as it was packed with zander. It was more or less one a chuck. Water conditions were nothing exceptional and the water was certainly not heavily coloured. The reason I think I had the big haul was because the zander population had just peaked in the Level and the food supply was starting to run out. The net result was that the zander were hungry and when any predator is hungry it can became easier to catch. I was later to catch a brace of pike from the same spot of 21 lb and 19 lb plus some more zander. Unfortunately, as quickly as it had come into existence the magic swim died completely. I have no idea why it was so good except that the fisheries survey that year did pick up a decent number of small fish particularly ruffe which may have been attracting the zander. Perhaps when those small fish had spread out or been eaten the zander moved out. Looking back over the years again quite recently, I dread to think the amount of fishing time I wasted going back to that spot.

The same year I had the best demonstration ever of how two dimensional Relief Channel fishing could be. Incidentally it was only a year after Dave Litton's 17 lb 12 oz zander from the Channel. The St Germans area continued to produce some good zander as it had done the year before. Regrettably some of the bigger fish had been killed and catching a double was no longer easy. My good friend Dave Moore was set up with his father Ben on the west bank with a brisk wind blowing over his head. I was diagonally opposite facing the wind. My ability to cast more than 30 yards was severely hampered by the wind, but in the end casting too far would have been a disadvantage. I had nineteen zander that day, the best being 9 lb while Dave, who could not reach them from where he was, had very little or even nothing. It was luck that I was on the east bank and it was even better luck that the zander were in front of me. Ever since then I have always had the tackle to enable me to fish both sides of the drain. These days with modern braid and powerful 3 lb test rods, distance is no longer a problem. Get yourself one of the Daiwa long cast reels and anything is possible. When I used braid and a long cast reel for the first time I had to stop the end tackle from hitting the far bank on the Channel. The next cast I had a bird's nest because I had over filled the reel. I quickly learned to limit the amount of line on the reel.

The zander fishing took a bit of a dive in the early 1980s what with prey fish population crashes and the infamous cull when tons of zander and pike were killed in order to re-establish a predator/prey fish balance. A lot of us hardened zander anglers decided to fish for something else. Some of us chose catfish in Bedfordshire drifting back to the zander fishing in the mid 1980s. We started fishing drains such as the River Delph and the Old Bedford and surprisingly I finally beat my personal best zander of 12 lb 10 oz set in 1970. The Old Bedford in particular was a lesson in never under estimating an unlikely looking water: 10 to 15 yards wide at most, very shallow with reedmace sticking out of the middle of the drain. The water was very coloured due to seepage of the silty tidal river water through the sluice at Salters Lode. I ended up, I think, with five or six doubles from a short stretch of drain, the best two being the same fish, the personal best, once at 15 lb 15 oz, a second time at a lesser weight but still a fifteen pounder though. These fish invariably came out at night which I presume was because of the shallowness of the water. The nearby Well Creek is a similar water, but unfortunately the Environmental Agency removed a lot of zander during survey

Zander fishing on the Relief Channel is two dimensional with a need for long casting.

Dave Litton and his 17 lb 12 oz zander caught from the Relief Channel in 1977; unfortunately it was killed.

work. That, however, was a long time ago and I cannot help wondering that this canal-type venue could be well worth fishing now.

The River Delph at the Welmore Sluice end was also very coloured in the mid eighties and it too produced some good zander. Even so, with the exception of one solitary fifteen pounder it was never as good as the Old Bedford. The Delph was not shallow so I bet there is a fair chance that zander can still be caught there.

Earlier I mentioned peg 13 at Stowbridge on the Relief Channel, and it is worth commenting that interesting things happened there as late as the 1990s. I picked up a thirteen pounder at night on a paternostered livebait, but a week later during daylight I was to be surprised by a zander grabbing a bait as I wound in. I actually saw the zander which in itself was exceptional. I was paternostering a live rudd fished head down on the trace. I was winding it in for a re-cast and the bait and lead had just come up over the marginal shelf when a zander of 7 lb appeared from nowhere and engulfed it. I landed this rather keen individual and remembered thinking how unusual this was. However, when you think about it, if you fish enough then almost anything that is unusual can actually happen; not very often of course but the more you fish the more likely it is to happen. Another trip years earlier in the same area saw the discovery of the benefit that could be gained by moving along the bank. I covered several hundreds of yards during the day and picked up zander from a number of spots along the way. I had without knowing it demonstrated what I later called 'semi-static' packs of zander. Zander were present dotted along the drain, interested in feeding but not prepared to move far to do so. When I moved to them I caught zander. On another day with the zander not prepared to feed my efforts would have been to no avail.

When I did my zander research at the University of Aston, as already hinted at I had to autopsy quite a few of the species. Amongst these were some fish from Coombe which were netted in December. They were packed with food despite it being very cold. The fact that we did not catch many zander in daylight suggested that they had to be feeding at night. I later proved this to myself on the Relief Channel catching zander quite easily at night when there was snow on the ground. The particular night in question did not yield any monsters but I did get a brace of six pounders so it was worth the effort. It was quite fun because snow tends to be quite dry when it is really cold. This was all part of the learning curve, I guess.

This cracking zander was caught at night in November on a livebait by Neville Fickling.

By 1990 I had realised many times that zander can be caught slap bang in the middle of the day. This makes for nice easy fishing and it gets even better if you can establish a pattern. On this particular day I was staying with the family in a house at Crimplesham not far from the Relief Channel and Middle Level. I had found a spot on the Middle Level that had in the old days been a surprisingly good pike spot. I never had a twenty from the swim though friends did. My best pike had been 19 lb 10 oz which is pretty close I am sure you agree. By 1990 the larger pike were a bit scarcer, but the zander fishing was getting better. The pattern I had spotted was that good zander would appear between about 11 am and 1 pm and if it was sunny then so much the better. Because early mornings had been a waste of time I drove over to Lincolnshire for a few hours pike fishing and I did not do badly with fish to 19 lb. I then battled my way back through Wisbech arriving at the Middle Level at about 10 am and following a five hundred yard walk I was there. I cannot remember exactly what happened, but I do remember getting a slim 13 lb zander on an eel section which is still my biggest from that particular drain. The fish came sometime in the early afternoon as the drain was pulling off slightly.

One thing I do enjoy about all coarse fishing is a 16 June success. Well for me that has always been a rare event, though once for a few years I had a swim on the Relief Channel that came up trumps more often than not. Naturally, because it was a good swim I enjoyed a few 16 June trips to it. I remember one summer evening casting out perhaps a tad before 16 June came around. I hoped that it would be the early hours before I had a run and this of course would be strictly legal. Unfortunately the zander had different ideas and I ended up landing a 12 lb 9 oz on an eel section the wrong side of midnight. As indicted previously, I am actually a strong supporter of the close season so I can honestly say I did not do that again.

Another 16 June in the 1990s was not illegal, but it was spectacularly successful. Only a couple of seasons earlier I had had a brace of double figure zander but on this trip I was to go one better and get a trio of doubles. The first one was a 12 lb on a dead-bait followed by a 10 lb on a livebait. The swim then died so I took a chance and moved seven hundred yards upstream to another reliable spot and picked up another 12 lb. The old spots were still producing then; unfortunately odd visits during the new millennium have not been so productive. To some extent this demonstrated to me the benefits of moving swims once one feels that the swim has been fished out. Of course you cannot tell what *might* have been caught if you had stayed, but I guess that is fishing for you.

Zander Waters

When it comes to waters that contain zander, the reader will not be surprised if I say it is impossible for me to, for instance, have the contact numbers at hand for all these waters. Having said this, the internet is very useful and you can certainly get current details about some fisheries by using Google. Having got that off my chest, the first choice club for all zander anglers has surely to be King's Lynn AA. They control so much of the best zander fishing that arguably not having one of their club books is just plain daft. For the 2007/8 season they worked out at £36 and this allows you to night fish which a day ticket does not.

The most famous of their waters has to be the Relief Channel which consists of eleven miles of water one hundred yards wide, most of which is hardly touched. To fish it though, you need to be fit unless you can put a boat on it prior to October, because otherwise you need to walk. The top end at Denver below the head sluice has always been worth a look. How fishable it is depends on how much water is flowing through. Downham Market Bridge is perhaps the most famous spot on the Channel because much of the action with zander during the early years was around here. The best areas are downstream of the bridge particularly the stones on the outside of the bend on the east bank. In fact, there is a road down the east side between the Channel and the railway line, and at the end is room for a couple of cars to park, this providing a useful short cut to the stones area.

Stowbridge is next along and lots of good zander have been caught within five hundred yards of either side of the bridge. There is also a pub there for the drinkers amongst you. A long way downstream is the mad mile; this is the mile above the old railway bridge. Access is poor though and the last time I was there, there were no gaps in the reed beds. Magdalen Bridge itself is not my favourite spot, but the next bridge down St Germans certainly had its day in the late 1970s. The magic area was about seven hundred yards up from the bridge. The rest of the Channel was not a lot of cop for zander, but to be honest you should never really say never, should you?

The other big water which ends near to King's Lynn is the Middle Level Drain. While until recently the zander record was still held by this water I was really surprised that another water had not stolen its crown much earlier. Still it is a very nice place to fish and I have had many happy days there, right from my tiddler catching days in 1961. It is a matter of opinion where the Middle Level ends and where the Sixteen Foot Drain starts. I always reckoned that the Level ended at Cottons Corner even though the drain from there to Three Holes is the same width as the Sixteen Foot. The junction between the drains at Three Holes was always worth a look, but I did better down towards Berries Bridge by the row of trees on the west bank. Next bridge down Pingle Bridge ought to be worth a try, but I was always cursed there. The Aqueduct is where the lower Level starts and it was always harder down from there, but the fish were bigger. There is no longer a bridge at Crooked Chimneys, but there is a track that leads to where it was. You can go upstream to near the wires or downstream between the non-existent Crooked Chimney Bridge and Morton's Bridge.

I think I had my first Level double downstream of Morton's, but by golly it is a long stretch to the next bridge at Neeps. Upstream of Neeps was always good as was halfway between Neeps and Rungays. I was not about much when the big ones were caught, the 18 lb and the 19 lb, but between Rungays and Magdalen was the area. Below Magdalen to the sluice was always even slower than anywhere else, but it did do a few sixteen pounders.

Steve Croll and a double figure Middle Level zander.

King's Lynn AA also have the Cut Off Channel from Denver up to the Wissington road bridge. People still zander fish it regularly, but it is rare to hear of any big ones these days. Lynn also has the Great Ouse at Ten Mile Bank which is fairly prolific for zander of all sizes and what is more the big advantage with the Ouse for the elderly or disabled is that the road runs alongside it.

Lynn also has a bit of the Little Ouse and the lower section of the Old Bedford. It is always worth keeping an eye on the Old Bedford, though it has suffered a series of 'natural' pollutions in recent years.

The Great Ouse between Southery and Earith regularly produces zander as does the Old West and the River Cam. There are certainly zander as far up as Wyboston because the lakes attached to the river produce them to the double figure mark. In Ely there are Roswell Pits of course, these once holding the zander record with an 18 lb 8 oz fish in 1988. At the moment though they are being developed and unfortunately this usually means bad news as far as the fishing is concerned.

The mystery water is the Hundred Foot River. This runs from Denver to Earith and is for much of its length tidal and very coloured. Zander do inhabit this water, but for some reason you never seem to hear of anyone fishing for them.

I mentioned the Delph earlier, and this twenty odd mile long drain has been quiet over recent years, but there is almost certainly plenty of scope there for a big zander. I remember Bryan Culley getting amongst the doubles on there years ago and I presume they are still there.

Over in Lincolnshire zander have spread to the River Nene and by flooding to Ferry Meadows Lake just to the west of Peterborough. The River Welland also has them and you can catch them in Spalding in the winter. Sometimes I even think it is safer to say that it is easier to say where there are no zander, rather than where they are.

Elsewhere around the country a good venue is the eighty acre Coombe Abbey Lake, Warwickshire. This council-owned lake has produced zander to 19 lb with a 19 lb 3 oz fish coming out in 1998. It also has a good website which gives all the details you will need. In the Leicester area are Frisby Pits and the pits near Birstall, while in Bedfordshire, there are Wyboston Pits. Zander are in the River Soar and, of course, the Trent itself. Furthermore, the entire English midlands canal network have them and British Waterways have now given up trying to remove them. Then there is the River Severn and although I have never fished it, Nige Williams does guided trips on the river and his customers have had zander to 14 lb (but also read about the new zander record below). The Warwickshire Avon was colonised by zander after the Severn, but is now producing fish over 15 lb.

Further south, old father Thames is also now a zander venue and these fish originally had nothing to do with the Thames at all. Old Bury Hill Lake in Surrey has a good reputation as a zander water. It did do some mid-double figure fish a while ago, but they are not being caught quite so big these days. Further south still Winton's Lake in Sussex has them, incidentally along with some monster catfish.

A magnificent 15 lb personal best zander for Mark Barrett.

So having briefly looked at some of the main zander waters, rather belatedly perhaps, a question that needs answering is what is a good zander? Well, as I mentioned earlier, my tackle is geared to catching fish of over 3 lb. But as we all know it depends on where you are fishing as to what might be considered a good fish. Let us look at somewhere like the Severn or Fens. To my mind a nice fish worthy of a session is a fish over 6 lb. Thereafter, a notable capture is a double and a fish over 13 lb is without doubt a very good fish with at the moment anything over 15 lb being very rare, though this did not stop Mark Barrett catching one! Having said that, we have certainly not seen the peak in size of the zander in Britain and they are destined to get bigger than 19 lb. If truth be told, soon after I wrote that last sentence, in July, 2007 the *Angling Times* reported that nineteen year old James Benfield had smashed the record by catching a 21 lb 5 oz monster from the River Severn. It was caught from the middle reaches of this mighty west midlands of England waterway and moreover it fell to a ledgered halibut pellet meant for bream. Dave Lavender's 1998 record of 19 lb 5 oz from the Middle Level had been well and truly obliterated. What is more James' previous best had only been 7 lb so after all, perchance there is hope for all of us.

In reality, as James Benfield's record shows, there is always a chance of that very special fish, whether it be a zander or any other freshwater predator. Going off at a tangent a little, here I am reminded by Steve Rogowski that he met three zander anglers at Roswell Pits in spring 2007. They were obviously mad keen and enthusiastic about their chosen quarry, also telling Steve they once took a friend, an occasional, non-specialist angler to the Middle Level in 1995. What is more this friend, a K Harter they said, had caught a magnificent 17 lb 5 oz zander on that trip, this being a fish that to this day remains in the top twenty of rod caught zander. But, despite this capture, Mr Harter has never been zander fishing again! That a K Harter caught such a fish is undoubtedly true but other than this, Steve is, not surprisingly, unsure of the authenticity or otherwise of what his alleged friends said. Even so, an important point remains: anyone, from the uninitiated, through to the beginner and more experienced angler, always has a chance of that zander fish of a lifetime.

In passing, prior to the aforementioned first 20 lb zander appearing, I thought that perhaps Grafham may well be a likely venue to produce a record breaker. They have certainly been present in that water long enough to have grown very big and I still await events here with interest but, after that Severn record breaker, I originally thought it would be a while before it was beaten. You can imagine my surprise, however, that as this chapter was being completed, the angling press reported rumours of a new record 24 lb zander from Grafham. Although the captor was unwilling to go public, perhaps time will eventually tell that I have been proved right after all.

Conclusion

There is a final point I want to end on, this being that, as I said at the outset, I like zander but it does make me sad and even angry that to my mind selfish individuals are spreading them around the waterways. Again as stated, they have even turned up in the Norfolk's River Yare. These illegal introductions do have a negative effect, not least in relation to pike, and they are irreversible. At the risk of being overly optimistic perhaps a more enlightened approach will emerge in the future and such antics will abate. Will this really occur though? Conceivably, but at the very least we can hope as well as wait and see. In the meantime, good luck to you all if you already do or intend to target zander. After all they are a very effective freshwater predator, and one that seems to be gaining in popularity at least as far as many freshwater predator anglers are concerned.

7
Challenges and Future Prospects
Steve Rogowski

At the present time there are many things to be positive about as far as pike and freshwater predator fish and fishing for them in the British Isles is concerned. Starting with pike, one has only to recall that during the 1950s and 1960s they were regarded as vermin and killed as such, or failing that killed for the table. In many areas during those days catching a 20 lb fish was a tall order indeed. Today generally such specimens seem to be more common, this in turn meaning many more of us have a chance of a biggie or two. Part of the explanation relates to the more enlightened attitude towards pike, together with better landing and unhooking techniques both of which can be put down to the campaigning activities of the Pike Anglers Club (PAC). Then again when it comes to catfish, perch and zander all three species are flourishing and there has never been a better time to catch them. Similar comments can be made in relation to such as chub and, on the whole, to trout.

However, everything in the garden is not all rosy when it comes to freshwater predator fish and in turn fishing for them. Trout can and are affected by pollution, over-abstraction of water and impeded access to spawning grounds. And the collapse of some sea trout populations in western Scotland and Ireland can be linked to salmon farming whereby the smolts have been lethally infested with sea lice transmitted from farmed salmon. Then again the salmon itself is threatened by over-exploitation by humans and once more by such as pollution and lack of access to spawning grounds, as well as general habitat degradation and reduced survival rates at sea.

But surely, as Steve Ormrod pointed out in his chapter, the freshwater predator fish that faces the most dangerous and uncertain future is the eel. There has been a major decline in the number of eels during the last two decades throughout Europe including the British Isles. As we will eventually see, the situation is such that the European Commission recognises the problems with eel replenishment, stocks and fisheries and is acting to protect the stock and safeguard fisheries for the future.

Apart from the problems and difficulties faced by specific species, particularly the eel, there are two other major challenges that angling in general as well as freshwater predator anglers in particular are going to have to face up to over coming years. First and foremost there is global warming and resulting changes in climate and weather to consider. Second, there is the anti-angling movement which, after its success in relation to helping to ban fox hunting in England, is increasingly likely to target angling

Thankfully, these days pike are generally not treated like this.

in its banning endeavours. And there are other subjects that are a concern such as the illegal capture and eating of freshwater fish which is a problem particularly in England, invasive species which pose a threat to native fish species, pollution and so on. All this is not an exhaustive list of course, but it does highlight some of the main issues that will have to be addressed.

This chapter begins with the challenges to pike and freshwater predator fishing in the British Isles. From all this, as well as the foregoing, the reader will be forgiven for thinking that the situation is, putting it mildly, rather bleak. However, I then look at future prospects and notwithstanding the very real and genuine concerns outlined, I end this book on an optimistic note arguing that overall the future remains positive as far as pike and freshwater predator fishing in the British Isles is concerned.

Current Challenges

In looking at some of the challenges to pike and freshwater predator fishing, there are, as the introduction to this chapter indicates, four main areas I want to consider. First, I look at the problems in relation to the decline of the eel. Second, I deal with global warming and climate change issues and the possible effects on freshwater predator fishing. Third, the anti-angling movement together with the challenges they pose to fishing for freshwater predators is addressed. And fourth, I tackle what might be termed miscellaneous challenges facing angling such as the illegal capture and eating of freshwater fish, invasive species and pollution.

The Decline of Eels

During the summer of 2007 the main BBC television news featured a story about the sad plight of the eel. One of the last Fenland eel netsmen told of how his nets used to be hard work to haul in because of the number and resultant weight of eels they contained. Unfortunately though this was no longer the case. The feature went on to explain that there has been a 95 per cent decline in the numbers of eels over the last twenty years and if this continues they are in very real danger of disappearing within the next five to ten years. As all anglers, or at least all predator anglers, will surely agree it really is a gloomy state of affairs.

I well recall eel fishing sessions as a child with my brother, our dad and his friend in the 1960s on the River Ure at Ripon. Long, warm summer evenings and into the night would produce lots of eels to the likes of ledgered worms and minnows. Even ten years ago you could catch them relatively easily but as I write this chapter, during the autumn of 2007, I have yet to catch an eel there this year. What is more I really miss them, no longer seeing them as I sometimes used to as a slimy pest, but rather as something to be prized and preserved. This was certainly the case, for example, when I

The poor eel is under severe pressure.

caught a 'bootlace' while worming for salmon on Northumberland's River Till; it was unhooked and returned to the river with care. Similar thoughts occurred when a little later I caught seven 'boots' plus a nice 1 lb plus eel on the River Ouse; again they were all returned unharmed. There is no doubt that the obvious question arises as to what has led to the eel's dramatic decline. In trying to provide an answer, again as Steve Ormrod mentioned, there are a number of factors to consider. Thus, there is overfishing, climate change, loss/degradation of freshwater habitat, bio-accumulation of chemicals and infection by parasites. I want to elaborate a little on some of these issues plus one other here.

As Alan Churchward and Jonathan Shelley note in Cynthia Davies *et al.*'s edited collection *Freshwater Fishes in Britain*, at all stages of its life the eel is exploited both in Europe and the British Isles. Glass eel and elver fisheries are found in the tidal reaches of the River Severn and other rivers flowing into the Bristol Channel. Yellow eels are caught using traps and nets in many areas especially East Anglia. Silver eels are taken using such as traps and fyke nets. In Britain elvers caught amounted to about ten tonnes a year and yellow and silver eels a few hundred tonnes. There is also the important elver fishery on the River Bann at Toomebridge, Northern Ireland, with many of these elvers being restocked elsewhere in the Bann catchment area, mainly Lough Neagh, for harvesting as yellow or silver eels. As well as eels being directly consumed by humans, the main market for elvers is the Far East for aquaculture. Meanwhile, on the Continent, most yellow eels are caught in mainland Europe and most silver eels in the Baltic Sea.

But it is not only over-exploitation that has had a bearing on eel stocks. It is equally likely that global warming and resulting climatic changes have had an influence. For instance, changes in the Gulf Stream can mean there is a vast reduction in the numbers of tiny elvers returning from the Sargasso Sea to our waters.

The eel has also certainly been affected by the loss of access to suitable freshwater habitat. Although they can certainly cross many barriers, including crossing land on damp nights, others such as weirs and tidal flaps can and do stop them reaching their habitat. Furthermore, apart from loss of access there is the degradation of their habitat to consider. Steve Ormrod points out that they are habitat sensitive. He once saw several eels up to the 3 lb mark trying to get away from a flooded Cheshire water by wriggling over rain sodden fields. At first he thought it was an exodus due to them returning to the sea to breed, but on realising that it was early July and that they were not morphing he knew that this was an unlikely scenario. He later discovered that a chemical had been added to the venue in order to control invasive weeds, and no doubt this had upset the eels which were most likely to have been trying to get to nearby lakes which had not been treated with the chemical.

There is little doubt that the introduction of a disease native to Japanese eels is another significant factor to consider. This disease is harmful, indeed fatal, to European eels because it involves the infection of the swim-bladder.

Finally, on a different tack over-predation is another factor in the eel's decline. By this I am not referring to the relatively few that may be eaten by such as pike, but rather the far larger numbers consumed by conservation species like the otter and the bittern. These are the types of animals and birds favoured by many animal lovers, unlike the eel which unfortunately for equally many is something to be loathed and despised.

All the above only goes to show that the decline of the eel is complex but nevertheless all would surely agree that the fish has a lot to contend with and it certainly is under a lot of severe pressure.

Global Warming and Climate Change

Moving to global warming, it may be stating the obvious but this is certainly something which has already and will continue to impact on planet Earth unless drastic action is taken. For example, ice caps will carry on melting, sea levels rising and climate and weather patterns changing, perhaps irreversibly. Despite the stubborn, delaying tactics of President Bush, scientific opinion, and the world as a whole, including belatedly the USA, have reached this consensus. In short, the planet is warming up as a result of the actions of mankind, not least the increased burning of fossil fuels over the last two hundred and fifty or so years. As far as the British Isles is concerned, winters are and will get wetter and milder, with gale force winds also becoming more frequent and less predictable. On the other hand, longer summers are likely to be hotter, drier and Mediterranean-like; witness the summer of 2006, for instance. All this is set to have a big impact on pike and freshwater predator fish and fishing for them. So why is global warming and climate change taking place and how is it likely to affect pike and freshwater predator fish and in turn angling for them?

Global warming and climate change are the result of the 'greenhouse effect'. The latter refers to the warming that happens when certain gases in the Earth's atmosphere trap heat. These gases let in light but keep heat from escaping, like the glass walls of a greenhouse. Thus, sunlight shines onto the Earth's surface where it is absorbed and then radiates back into the atmosphere as heat. In the atmosphere 'greenhouse' gases trap some of this heat while the rest escapes into space. The more greenhouse gases there are in the atmosphere, the more heat is trapped and the planet warms up. Scientists have known about the greenhouse effect since the early nineteenth century, and in 1895 the Swedish chemist Arrhenius discovered humans could enhance the effect by making carbon dioxide which they have increasingly done by, as stated, burning fossil fuels since the Industrial Revolution. All this has led to the global warming and climate changes we are witnessing today. Admittedly average global temperatures and concentrations of carbon dioxide have fluctuated on a cycle of hundreds of thousands of years, but humans have increased this gas, and resultant changes, by a staggering one third since the Industrial Revolution. All this is the key to the problems we are now experiencing.

As for wetter, milder winters, I seem to recall that it was during the winter of 2000

Steve Rogowski surveying a drought-stricken reservoir. Hotter, drier summers are likely to lead increasingly to scenes like this.

that there were days of heavy, persistent rain with resultant severe flooding in various parts of the British Isles including the River Ouse around York. The situation was such that many residential areas were under water and suffered flood damage. Thereafter, checking my records the Ouse does seem to be flooding more regularly. Admittedly, all the Yorkshire Dales' rivers flow into the Ouse so it has always been prone to flooding, but surely global warming and climate change are additional factors to consider.

Having written the foregoing about winter flooding and also the point about hotter, drier summers, one has only to recollect the summer of 2007 which turned out to be literally a washout. In June persistent, heavy rain caused severe flooding over much of northern England especially south Yorkshire and Humberside with Sheffield, Rotherham, Barnsley, Doncaster and Hull all being severely affected. At one stage the M1 motorway was blocked as in some areas two months of rain fell in twelve hours. Such weather was repeated in July but this time in Herefordshire, Worcestershire and Gloucestershire especially at Tewkesbury where the rivers Avon and Severn converge. The town was virtually cut off and water supplies were disrupted as treatment centres were flooded. Then again Reading and Oxford also suffered as the River Thames in Oxfordshire and Berkshire rose dramatically. Overall although wetter, milder winters

193

Because of increased flooding are we going to see more signs like this?

and hotter drier summers are to be expected, more erratic, dramatic and extreme weather changes will also occur.

Further afield one has only to recall, for example, the increased hurricane activity in the Caribbean culminating in Katrina which devastated New Orleans, and as I write there are floods in west and east Africa in such as Ghana and Sudan where desert conditions are the norm. In addition, as this book was being completed there were extreme floods in the southern Mexican state of Tobasco.

The changes that have and are taking place will provide unique challenges to all life: plant, animal as well as human. According to the Environment Agency, temperature changes alone can have direct effects on fish stocks. For example, a rare fish, the schelly, which dates back to the Ice Age, was recently found dead in Ullswater in the English Lake District. It only lives in cold, deep water and global warming will certainly make life more difficult for this species in the future. Another obvious example, and closer to home for the readers of this book, is that higher sea temperatures have, as indicated, adversely affected eel as well as salmon migration routes in the north Atlantic.

Higher rainfall can also impact adversely on eggs in trout and salmon redds as well as on the eggs of many coarse, including predator, fish more generally, simply by washing them away. Or again, juveniles of all such fish could lose their riffle, shallow water, habitat. In fact, it was not long after the already referred to Ouse flood of 2000 that I noticed that there was a decline in the number of pike, especially large pike, that I was catching there. Perhaps that particular flood, and increased floods thereafter, had something to do with this. Other experienced pike anglers seemed to agree also saying that at the very least the floods had torn up old trees and big snags that held pike, so that they were no longer in such swims. Although my Ouse pike captures have picked up a little of late they certainly do not match my 20 lb fish captures of the 1990s.

Flooding can also have disastrous effects on pike fishing in other ways especially when Government flood defence cuts come into play. For example, in early 2007 the Environment Agency's Anglian Regional Flood Defence Committee was told that its budget for the following year would be cut by 5.2 million pounds. The shortfall meant that work on building up beaches between Eccles and Winterton, on the north-east Norfolk coast, would not go ahead thereby leaving Horsey Mere and the Upper Thurne dangerously vulnerable to sea water surges which in turn could easily become more common. The Thurne system, of course, occupies a unique place in pike fishing history having produced record pike of over 40 lb. Some experts predict that villages like Hickling and Waxham, not to mention 6000 hectares of the Broads themselves and fishing thereon are under huge threat.

When it comes to hotter, drier summers, these can have a number of possible negative consequences. First, they could lead to, for example, pike and perch spawning

Pike and perch spawning areas, together with their eggs, could be left high and dry in such reservoirs.

areas in and around marginal vegetation and aquatic plant life being left high and dry in stillwaters such as reservoirs. Second, it is important to note that pike themselves do not usually tolerate high temperatures, say above 30°F, which can often prove fatal. And third, as Chris Bishop points out in *PAC30: A Celebration of 30 Years of the Pike Anglers Club of Great Britain* as water becomes a scarce commodity in such as the drought-hit south-east of England, water abstraction will increase. An example is the proposal for water from the Great Ouse being used to fill an enlarged Abberton Reservoir, Essex which in turn may prohibit fishing there in the future.

All-in-all global warming and climate change will have an effect on pike and freshwater predator fish and angling for them in the British Isles, but I now turn to another key challenge to such fishing in these countries namely the anti-angling movement.

The Anti-Angling Movement

The anti-angling movement (AAM), linked to the more broadly based animal rights activists, has been prominent for many decades. One of their most prominent successes, as indicated, was to help ban fox hunting and this success is likely to increase their confidence and determination this time in relation to banning angling itself. One has only to look at the internet to see how determined they are. Admittedly there is some, perhaps half-hearted, acknowledgement that, for example, anglers are conservationists and do some good by putting pressure on polluters. They also tend to accept that anglers monitor the waterways and generally manage fisheries quite well. But these positives are far outweighed by their general anti-angling stance which amounts to a propaganda war and includes, for instance, giving detailed advice on how to contact the press and deal with the media about anti-angling issues, together with even how to achieve a local authority ban on angling. Furthermore, as in all propaganda, much of what they say regarding angling is either factually incorrect or exaggerated. For example, they talk of anglers' lead weights causing pollution, playing down or ignoring the fact that they are no longer used and nor have they been for some time. Or again they talk of 'litter pollution' caused by anglers, neglecting to say that this is something that the vast majority of anglers also abhor and moreover such anglers do everything they can to educate and persuade the irresponsible culprits.

But probably the main argument the AAM uses is in relation to fish and pain, this being particularly relevant as far as livebaiting is concerned. It goes without saying that livebaiting is one of the main methods in the freshwater predator anglers' armoury. The AAM does acknowledge that anglers do have a strong argument when it comes to the issue of fish feeling pain. This is that, bearing in mind animals, including fishes, tend to avoid anything that gives them a painful sensation, the fact that fish eat shellfish and other spiky objects means their mouths simply cannot feel pain. One has only to recall that pike love perch and ruffe despite their spiny dorsal fins. Despite this acknowledgement, the AAM goes on to use very emotive language when it talks about fish and pain. Thus, fish are said to be 'deceived into impaling' themselves on hooks,

As Steve Rogowski points out, if the anti-angling movement has its way there will be more signs like this.

of being 'worn out' before they are landed, of being 'dragged into a suffocating, alien environment' and so on. Also, they argue, despite the earlier comments, that as fish are vertebrates with a brain 'it is common sense they feel pain'. Such factors, the argument goes, means angling should be banned.

However, if we look at all the anti-angling arguments in a more objective, scientific way, then the situation is far from clear. You can, of course, find some scientists who do argue that fish feel pain and even fear when caught by an angler. However, there are other scientists who at the very least are wary of linking human emotions such as pain and fear to less complex animals and organisms like fish. To feel such emotions, they argue, a being must be conscious and aware, but as fish only have very small brains they therefore have no conceptual system capable of doing this. In a nutshell, we should be aware of anthropomorphism, that is, attributing human qualities to fish. What is more, as Neville Fickling puts it in Bob Church's *Big Pike*, 'all the evidence is that fish do not feel pain as we know it'. He also adds, more colloquially and amusingly, that after catching the same pike on the same bait three times on the same day 'aversion therapy does not work for pike, at least' (p101 to 102).

Despite the last paragraph, it is likely that the anti-angling movement will be a thorn in the side of angling in general and, because of such as livebaiting, freshwater predator fishing in particular, for many years to come.

197

Miscellaneous Challenges

When it comes to what I have termed miscellaneous challenges, as suggested there are three main ones that I want to deal with here. These are the illegal capture and eating of freshwater fish including predator fish, invasive species and pollution.

Beginning with the illegal capture and eating of fish, barely a week seems to go by these days without one reading about it in the angling press. It usually features stories about how this is done by immigrants from Eastern Europe following the expansion of the European Community. There have been recent reports about such as carp and bream being taken from Church Pool at Tong, as well as other species from the River Penk, both in Shropshire. Following this an online petition calling for the Government to act was started. Meanwhile in Kent crude fishing tackle as well as nets and traps were being used to catch eels, roach and crayfish from Nickolls Quarry, Palmarsh, on the Isle of Sheppey, a lake in Kemsley and the River Bourne. There was also a separate incident on the Shropshire Union Canal at Autherley when eastern Europeans were found with dead bream in plastic bags. And on some of the reservoirs in north-west England that I tackle for pike I have also heard stories of nightlines with numerous baited hooks being set with again the spotlight falling on eastern Europeans.

But surely one must remember it is not only foreigners that are hoping to catch fish for the pot. I recall Matt Hayes reporting on how parts of the lower reaches of the Rivers Severn and Avon have banks lined with caravans and houseboats many of their occupants fishing for zander and, less so, pike mainly to eat. These people were certainly not eastern Europeans.

At this stage there are two points I wish to make in relation to all the above. First, when it comes to illegal fishing it is not always about fishing for the pot by foreigners that should be the focus of attention. In particular, what about all those native licence dodgers that we hear relatively little about? Why is there little apparent concern about them? As is often the case in our society, it is the foreigner who is made the scapegoat for our ills. In addition, I guess we have all heard stories, or indeed know for a fact, about poachers, again mainly if not exclusively native, who target specimen fish, usually carp, with a view to transporting them to other waters where they are paid a substantial sum. Second, the police and Environment Agency simply do not have the resources to deal with all the complaints/crimes reported to them. Burdened by Government targets and paperwork, together with, it must be said, the far more serious crimes that are committed it is no wonder they are often unable to act. I know it is one of my hobby-horses, and that this might be controversial for some, but if we really want to make sure that these and other public servants are genuinely able to do what we want them to, then we have to be willing to pay for them in the form of higher taxes, particularly from those who are more well off. But even though some might find such views controversial, the key point is surely that despite some illegal fishing, including some for the pot by foreigners, we should all surely please keep this in perspective.

Turning to invasive species, of those that are currently affecting the British Isles, perhaps the most significant is the American signal crayfish, *Pacifastacus leniusculus*. Simon Clarke and Mark Barrett have already referred to this menace in their chapters on catfish and perch respectively, and I first came across them in Loch Ken a few years ago. A local man told me that someone hoped to breed them so they could be used in restaurants but that they accidentally escaped into the River Dee and the loch itself. In fact, they were originally imported to Britain in the 1970s to be commercially bred for food and established themselves in numerous river systems in southern Britain. Only recently Peter Hague, an experienced pike and specimen angler, was at pains to tell me about his concerns if they spread on the Keighley Anglers' stretch of the River Aire and other Yorkshire rivers. They are certainly now in Loch Ken and other waters in south-west Scotland and even in a few further north. As far as Ken is concerned I have even been told by roach fishers that the situation is so bad that on occasions they are catching as many signals as roach. They even cling on to swimfeeders, simply refusing to let go and can be landed in this manner.

The problem with signals is that they are more robust and aggressive than our native version and outcompete them in terms of breeding and food. They also spread 'crayfish plague' which is fatal, not to them, but native crayfish. What is more they can climb and walk considerable distances thereby taking over waters formerly inhabited by native crayfish. They can burrow several feet into river banks thereby

An American signal crayfish claw on the banks of Loch Ken.

actually undermining them. They also damage plant and invertebrate life as well as fish. Indeed, they are likely to have a disastrous effect on many fish stocks particularly because they prey on small fish and fish eggs. There is even some evidence that they can exclude juvenile salmon from sheltered water in winter thereby increasing the vulnerability of salmon to predators. Further, they can make fishing for pike a real toil as most ledgered baits are very quickly and literally stripped to the bone.

Here it is worth mentioning two other crayfish species that potentially pose serious problems. First, Turkish crays have been found in the River Waveney and as well as spreading 'crayfish plague' they pose similar problems as the signals. Second, there is the marble crayfish, thought to be of North American origin, which can reproduce asexually so that one individual can establish a whole population. Both could have a devastating impact on plant, invertebrate and, not least, fish life.

Another invasive species is the topmouth gudgeon, *Pseudorasbora parva*, introduced into Britain in the 1980s by a supplier of ornamental fishes. They originate from the far east in such as China, Japan, Korea and the Amur basin and were first seen over here in stillwaters in Hampshire, then Buckinghamshire and Staffordshire, before most recently being found in Cheshire, Cumbria and other areas. The spread is probably due to unintentional transfers as it is difficult to distinguish these fish from other small cyprinids. They are highly invasive because of their broad range of environmental tolerance limits and rate of reproduction; they can actually breed four times a year. Furthermore, they are a real threat to native species, including freshwater predator fish, because of their direct predation on eggs and the competition they provide for other prey items. Finally, they also carry a parasite that could affect native fish thereby leading to devastating environmental consequences. The Environment Agency has had to eradicate this pest in Cumbria by poisoning but, of course, this killed all the other fish present and the water had then to be restocked from scratch.

Moving to pollution, the days of the Industrial Revolution have long gone as far as the British Isles are concerned. From my childhood in the 1950s and 1960s I can recall polluted Yorkshire rivers such as the Aire, Calder and Don but they have certainly been cleaned beyond recognition over recent decades. This is evidenced by the return of salmon to some of these waters. Similar comments can be made about other rivers such as the Trent, Mersey, Tyne, Wear and, in Scotland, the Clyde. Mention of the Mersey reminds me that the Environment Agency has reported that barbel have been found there for the first time in living memory. And again, in a different vein, the improvement in water purity is evidenced by the fact that although lampreys have been in decline they are now making a recovery, a good example being in the River Tamar on the Devon/Cornwall border; the Environment Agency have recently recorded five times more than the seasonal average. Similar comments can be made about the revival of the otter; again it was Peter Hague who told me about his sightings on the River Aire around Keighley. However, despite all these positive developments there are other things to be concerned about. Pollution from traditional industry may be a thing of the past but new forms of pollution are taking its place.

Not so long ago I recall reading about several freshwater fish species changing sex because of chemicals being released into rivers, not least those involved in the making of the contraceptive pill; even the disposal of unused contraceptive pills down toilet systems was said to be linked to this. Then there is the ever increasing use of chemicals in agriculture to consider, as surely the leeching of such chemicals into rivers and stillwaters is bound to have some effect on fish stocks. For example, there are current concerns about the average size of pike in Bassenthwaite which is now down to 12 lb. Naturally, being top of the fish food chain, the size of pike is a good indicator of the health of the lake. Indeed, early in 2007 the Environment Agency reported that a third of Britain's lakes were affected by over-exploitation by humans, the biggest threat being the enrichment of water by nutrients, nitrogen and phosphates as a result of increased agricultural land use. The constant need for new housing and resultant pressure on drainage and sewage systems is another factor to consider. Recently pike were among the thousands of fish killed when sewage polluted the River Wandle a tributary of the

River Thames. But it is not only populated areas of England, especially in the south and south-east, that one must be concerned about. If you take Ireland, for example, as Mark Ackerley has pointed out, Lough Corrib has its problems; water quality in lower Corrib is less than it should be because of the concentration of sewage as a result of the increase in numbers of houses on its banks here. One consequence is the poor condition of the pike which often tend to be lean and lice infected. In contrast pike at the head of the Corrib system, where there is far less housing development, are better conditioned, and are fat and lice-free. It is not just the Republic of Ireland that has its problems though. In the north the Lough Neagh system suffered a pollution incident resulting in many fish being killed in January 2007. And three months later, leakage of 8000 litres of red diesel into Lough Beg caused devastation to fish, including pike, and wildlife. This is all made even worse when one considers that Lough Beg is a Site of Special Scientific Interest.

Brian Steele returns a 3 lb perch to the canal but note the signs of pollution.

201

It is easy to see pike and freshwater predator fish themselves, and in turn angling for them, do have much to put up with: illegal fishing, whether for the table or not, the spread of invasive species and the threats from pollution. Having looked at these miscellaneous challenges, along with the other, more specific challenges referred to earlier in this chapter, if we look to the future perhaps, however, it is not all doom and gloom as I hope the following section shows.

Future Prospects

The challenges to pike and freshwater predator fish means that for those who love or who are passionate about angling for them, it is easy to feel a sense of despair. The decline of the eel perhaps epitomises what could face pike and many of the freshwater predator fishes of the British Isles. In turn it could well mean the decline of our sport at least as far as this area of the world is concerned. But my argument is that such a view, such pessimism, ought to be resisted not least because it fails to take into account possible ways forward, ways of responding to these very challenges. This is what I hope to examine and convey here as I revisit the decline of the eel, global warming and climate change, the anti-angling movement and the miscellaneous challenges referred to.

The Eel

Beginning with the eel, while acknowledging that the species is in a very serious predicament, steps are being taken to address the situation. In the first place, the European Commission does recognise the problem and as a result is organising the establishment of a programme of research, monitoring and direct action with the aim of helping eels to recover. As far as England is concerned, for example, the Environment Agency has looked at the eel's life cycle and the conditions they need for migration up rivers. This has included a review of existing eel passes including their design, location and effectiveness which in turn will eventually enable new fish passes to be created. In addition, during early spring 2007 the Agency released almost 70,000 elvers into Yorkshire's River Aire and a lake at a nature reserve near Chesterfield. I also well recall a senior Agency officer saying that '[we want] to protect this exceptional fish and save their populations from the catastrophic collapse we have seen over recent years'. It goes without saying that I, along with all who are keen on freshwater predator fishing, wholeheartedly agree.

Then again, the writer and broadcaster Hugh Fearnley-Whittingstall has referred to modern technology of fish farming helping the eel. He rightly notes the concerns of the industry to help solve problems in relation to wild fish stocks, and apparently they have even achieved the captive spawning of eels, followed by successful fertilisation and hatching. The next problem is how to nurture the larvae through the first year or two of life and into the elver stage, and developments here are awaited with interest. If this breakthrough were to be achieved the commercial pressures on wild eel stocks

Steve Rogowski is happy to catch and release this young eel caught on Northumberland's River Till.

could be relieved. Furthermore, captive-bred eels could be used to restock our lakes and rivers, and what a boost that would certainly be. A key question though is whether such eels could ever find their way back to the Sargasso Sea and breed naturally. Overall perhaps there are still more questions than answers.

Finally, for what it is worth, I would also add that after a few years of barely catching an eel, at least my catches, in terms of numbers at least, have increased over the last year or so. You cannot really conclude anything from one angler's catch rate of course, but I do really hope it augers well for the future of eels and eel fishing.

Climate Change

Global warming and climate change is undoubtedly the greatest challenge facing humanity and will remain so, at least for the rest of this century and into the next as well. We in the rich west, the ones responsible for causing the phenomenon, surely have to lead the way in addressing the situation. Sir Nicholas Stern, former chief economist at the World Bank, points out that if we do not spend large sums of money now on measures to reduce carbon emissions, economic and social disruption will take place on a massive scale. Furthermore, even if governments were to do what he advocates, that is reducing carbon emissions, for the foreseeable future global warming and climate change will continue on the lines sketched earlier in this chapter.

203

Accordingly, as far as the reader's and my lifetime are concerned, we are, to be blunt, stuck with such changes. As far as pike and freshwater predator fishing in the British Isles is concerned some of the negative effects have already been referred to. But, perhaps surprisingly, there are some positives.

For example, and despite my earlier comments about the possibility of their spawning areas drying out in such as reservoirs, as Mark Barrett told *Angling Times* in his role as general secretary of the Pike Anglers Club, pike are found in such as France and Spain, so overall warmer, drier summers may well not pose a major problem for them. Incidentally it occurs to me that similar comments could be made about perch and zander. Or again, as Steve Ormrod points out in his chapter, warmer winters may well be good for eel fishing, while in a similar vein Simon Clarke notes in his contribution that catfish in southern Britain are at their northernmost limits, but if the climate becomes warmer surely they will be able to survive in northern Britain as well. So, given the undoubted problems that global warming and climate change will bring, perhaps, albeit from a rather parochial stance, there are at least some positives to look forward to as well.

Despite the challenges from global warming, pike, perch and zander, along with catfish, could all do well. Here we have (ABOVE): Steve Rogowski with an 18 lb 8 oz reservoir pike; (RIGHT): Mark Goddard with a nice River Ouse perch; and Mark Barrett with an 11 lb 11 oz River Delph zander.

Anti-angling

When it comes to the anti-angling movement, if anything I am more ambivalent about future possibilities here. Admittedly, angling remains the largest participatory sport in the British Isles so it would surely be foolhardy for any politician to attempt to ban it. In addition, New Labour has repeatedly said they have no such plans in this area. Nevertheless, events like the Iraq war, together with New Labour's betrayal of those it is supposed to represent, namely the trade unions, will lead many to believe that the party cannot be trusted. And in my view the Tories certainly cannot be trusted in this, or in any other area for that matter. In addition, one has only to note the growth and increased influence of the animal rights movement, linked to the anti-angling movement of course, which could eventually mean that calls to ban angling cannot so easily be dismissed. As a result pike and freshwater predator anglers, indeed anglers as a whole, need to more vocal and organised in the years, even decades, to come.

Echoing Chris Bishop's views, again in *PAC30*, predator groups like the Pike Anglers Club (PAC), Catfish Conservation Group, National Anguilla Club, Perch-fishers, and Zander Anglers Club, together with such as the Salmon and Trout Association, need to adopt a more activist approach and confront issues and potential threats in a well-argued, professional way. Bridges and links also need to be made with the conservation movement especially the well-funded and powerful bird lobby to ensure anglers are properly acknowledged as stakeholders in the environment. For example, on the Isle of Wight constructive talks between local anglers and the Royal Society for the Protection of Birds led to the latter renewing access to the only river fishing on the island on the River Yar. One has only to recall that pikers and freshwater predator anglers in general, indeed like all anglers, are surely naturalists and ecologists with a deep understanding and concern for their environment. Finally, alliances also need to be forged with groups like the Specialist Anglers Alliance (SAA) and the Fisheries and Conservation Trust so as to present a united voice to those with power to help us safeguard pike and freshwater predators and fishing for them. Incidentally, as I write, several more broadly based angling bodies – for example, the National Federation of Anglers and the National Association of Fisheries and Angling Consultatives – have come together with a view to fighting the threats to angling like pollution and water abstraction, and fish theft. Interestingly though, there appears to be no direct mention of anti-angling issues or for that matter other concerns like global warming/climate change. Having written that last sentence though, the angling press has just reported that a coalition of conservation groups have slammed the Government for not making England and Wales more water-friendly and more secure against the extremes of drought and floods. Perhaps after all the tide is beginning to turn.

Furthermore, and related to freshwater predator fishing more directly, a fine example of what can be achieved occurred in early 2007 when the Environment Agency, after consulting with such as the PAC and SAA announced that the livebaiting ban would not be extended in England and Wales. This only goes to show you what can be

Remaining steadfast in the face of anti-angling propaganda ensures we can still catch pike like this: Steve Rogowski with a nice River Ouse double.

achieved if the aforementioned strategies and tactics are adopted. It is only in so doing that pike and freshwater predator fishing is likely to win through.

Albeit in a different vein, but also showing what can be achieved, another success worth commenting upon relates to the River Wandle pollution incident referred to above. As a result of pressure from angling and conservation groups, Thames Water apologised and accepted full responsibility for what occurred with their chief executive promising to compensate those affected and to not only restore but to actually improve the river. In fact, compensation subsequently totalled half a million pounds and one result is that thousands of chub, dace, barbel and roach have been restocked into the river. Then again pike anglers and conservationists have recently won the fight to save Cambridgeshire's historic lodes. These carry water across low-lying fens into the River Cam. Their future has been under review but the Environment Agency have recently agreed that the lodes will be repaired and so water levels will be maintained on these important pike fisheries for the next five years at least. All this followed an online petition by the parties referred to, not least Dennis Moules who is the PAC's Anglian liaison officer. Naturally this success is to be welcomed but I also suggest that we be aware of the five years' reprieve and prepare for another battle in 2012.

Illegal Fishing

The illegal capture of fish, including pike and freshwater predators, for the table is currently a major concern. Although I recognise the damage that such fishing can do to such fish stocks, I maintain, as stated, that a sense of perspective should prevail in this debate. Repeating what I said earlier, illegal fishing by natives, either by not having a rod licence or poaching carp to locate elsewhere, has also to be addressed. But illegal fishing for the table, currently the main moral panic, warrants further consideration.

There is no doubt that some do take pike and such as eels, perch and zander for the table and therefore there is a problem. But key questions arise as to the extent of the problem and what responses should be made to it. James Holgate, the respected pike angler and writer, has neatly summarised the arguments in *Pike and Predator* magazine. Like him I have no problem with any angler taking a small pike, a perch or zander to eat, and to be honest this is something I occasionally do. Likewise, Neville Fickling acknowledges in his zander chapter that he has taken them for the pot on occasions.

Michael Rogowski likes to catch jacks (though always hoping for a biggie!) like this on Mepps-like spinners, also taking the odd one for the pot; surely we cannot object to this.

One has also only to recall that during the Middle Ages pike or luce as it was called was considered a delicacy, as it, along with perch and zander, still are in parts of Eastern Europe. Even lamprey were considered a delicacy and King Henry I is said to have died from eating too many!

Moreover, and rather obviously, trout and salmon are eaten as a matter of course. In fact, can we, as pike and freshwater predator anglers who use dead and livebaits, have any real moral objection to the killing of any fish on any occasion? The answer is obviously no and surely the real concern is the uncontrolled – either by method, season, numbers or size – taking of pike and other freshwater predator fish. A distinction then ought to be made between an occasional fish killed to eat, and fish needlessly slaughtered either by ignorant match anglers or immigrants fishing illegally. And in the case of the latter two scenarios, surely education and persuasion are the ways forward rather than the heavy-handed use of the law. For example, this could include visiting farms where migrant workers are employed and putting up notices and giving out leaflets in several languages, explaining that stealing fish is an offence and anyone caught could be liable to prosecution. In fact, I understand that such strategies as this are currently being put in place. And surely, this ought to deter many even though the law cannot realistically be applied in every case because of the financial and resource difficulties mentioned earlier in relation to such as the police and Environment Agency.

Invasive species

When it comes to invasive species, in many respects often there is very little that can be done other than try and prevent their proliferation. There would certainly seem to be little chance of eradicating them completely. Take the signal crayfish: my view is that they are destined to stay and spread, and we simply have to get used to having them. Perhaps it is a little like the introduction of the zander which was seen as a great threat to native fish species when it was first released into the Fenland waterways. But nature has ways of dealing with such introductions and now, as we all know, zander are a prized, sought after quarry. Returning to the signal crayfish, we may even get to like and value them too, especially as they do make very good eating. And as for them stripping ledgered pike baits, one remedy is to use eels which the signals do not seem to like. I also thought that this would apply to the use of lamprey too. However, after a recent trip to Loch Ken my so-called theory was, quite simply, wrong! I used ledgered lamprey section on two rods for most of one day, catching a jack on one of them. But on pulling the rods in at the end of the day, one was completely baitless and the other only had a badly mangled piece of lamprey skin on it; the signals had certainly been enjoying themselves. Another way of 'defeating' them though is, of course, to pop-up or paternoster your baits. Similarly, if you are targeting perch then keeping your baits off the bottom could be the answer. Equally signals are not all bad news because, as Mark Barrett writes in his chapter, Great Ouse perch seem to like them and are growing to specimen size in increasing numbers as a result. Similarly, in his contribution Simon Clarke noted that catfish also feed on them, as do chub.

As for the topmouth gudgeon, there is some hope that these can be controlled, even eradicated, without having to poison them and all the other fish in the water. This is because more recently the Environment Agency has successfully used bio-manipulation techniques on a stillwater in the Wirral. Thus, in February 2006 a small number of mature perch were introduced in the hope they would prey on the invaders and control their numbers naturally. Sure enough a netting in October revealed the topmouth and their fry were at the lowest levels seen in the water, and what is more the perch had had a successful breeding season. Hopefully, such bio-manipulation will

Popping up/paternostering your baits or using eel sections means you avoid dreaded signal crayfish, and like Bill Palmer can catch a beautifully marked river pike .

Plump and immaculate – not Richard Young but his fine Yorkshire river, crayfish-liking, chub!

be the way forward for dealing with this pest as well as with any others that may arise in the future.

Pollution

Pollution in our rivers and stillwaters may be far less than it was during the Industrial Revolution, but as indicated earlier it continues to be a problem. The answer to this, despite previous comments about resource implications, would seem to be to enforce the law rigorously and ensure that the culprits are tracked down and severely punished. Unfortunately, and despite what occurred in relation to Thames Water and the River Wandle, it seems to be all too often that we hear about companies being fined in effect a pittance after causing untold damage to fish, other aquatic life and the environment in general. This has to change even though it seems the main political parties always bend over backwards to ensure the views and interests of big business hold sway. Despite this, and tying in with some of Chris Bishop's earlier comments, pollution is certainly something that pike and freshwater predator fishing organisations, as well as angling and conservation organisations more generally could and should be far more vociferous about.

Conclusion

To conclude this book then, it has to be acknowledged pike and freshwater predator fishing in the British Isles has certainly come a long way in the almost sixty years of my life. No longer are pike, and even zander, treated deplorably and 'knocked on the head' often not even for the table. Though problems still arise from time to time – you sometimes hear calls from match fishers for the culling of pike and zander from certain waters, for example – overall this is not the case now. Fishing for such freshwater predators, along with catfish and perch has come on leaps and bounds; all are now generally accepted as genuine sporting fishes. In many ways, and despite the challenges referred to throughout this chapter, there has never been a better time to fish for them along with chub and trout. Unfortunately, the same cannot be said about the eel and, less so, the salmon but even here perhaps there is some hope for the future as I hope I have shown.

In addition, one has only to recall that pike and freshwater predator fishing is one of relatively few forms of angling that retains an element of real mystery, excitement and anticipation. Not least it carries with it the heart stopping uncertainty of not knowing what the next capture will bring. When the float gives that first tell-tale shudder and bob, or the drop-off indicator trembles and falls while the alarm bleeps, who is to know whether the result will be weighing in at 1 lb or specimen size? Such fishing as this can also be a welcome antidote to more sanitised forms of angling, as it can take us to wild, unfished places as we explore remote areas of our rivers or stillwaters. In so doing we may well get freezing hands and feet, along with getting wet and downhearted as we become covered in rain and snow. Or in contrast we may swelter in the hot summer sun. But what can beat catching a big pike, catfish, eel, perch or zander, and chub, trout and salmon too, all of which form an impressive sight, this being made all the more exciting by knowing you are looking at a wild creature?

Remember though, that such freshwater predator fish should be respected and treated with care. This is particularly so when landing, unhooking and returning your quarry to the water. Simply put, you must make sure all this is done as quickly as possible so that any stress and harm to the fish is minimised. By so doing it ensures you show respect to these magnificent creatures, and in turn you help to preserve the sport of pike and freshwater predator fishing in the British Isles for generations to come.

Tight lines and tight braids, in short good luck to all you pike and freshwater predator anglers everywhere!

References and Further Reading

Bailey J. and Miller R. (1989) *Perch: Contemporary Days and Ways* Crowood Press
Bailey J. and Page M. (1985) *Pike: The Predator Becomes the Prey* Crowood Press
Barrett M. (forthcoming) *Zander Fishing: A Complete Guide* Crowood Press
Berners J. (1496) *A Treatyse of Fysshynge wyth an Angle*
Brown M. (1993) *Pike: The Practice and the Passion* Crowood Press
Brown M. et al (2006) *The Fox Guide to Modern Pike Fishing* Fox International Group
Buller F. and Falkus H. (1988) Second Edition *Freshwater Fishing* Clay's Ltd
Catfish Conservation Group (2005) Second Edition *Guide to UK Catfish Waters* CCG
Church B. (2006) *Big Pike* Crowood Press
Crawford L. (2006) *Trout Fishing in the UK and Ireland* Swan Hill Press
Davies C. et al (2004) *Freshwater Fishes in Britain: The Species and Their Distribution* Harley
    Books
Falkus H. *Salmon Fishing* Witherby
Fickling N. (1982) *Pike Fishing in the 80s* Freshwater Publishing
Fickling N. (1986) *In Pursuit of Predatory Fish* Beekay
Fickling N. (1992) *Pike Fishing with Neville Fickling* Freshwater Publishing
Fickling N. (2002) *Everything You Need to Know About Pike Fishing* Lucebaits Publishing
Fickling N. (2004) *Mammoth Pike* Lucebaits Publishing
Fickling N. and Rickards B. (1979) *Zander* A&C Black
Fort T. (2003) *The Book of Eels* Harper Collins
Golder J. (1983) *Top Ten* Beekay
Gustafson P. (2006) Second Edition *How to Catch Bigger Pike from Rivers, Lochs and Lakes* Swan
    Hill Press
Guttfield F. (1978) *The Big Fish Scene* Ernest Benn
Hansen J. P. and Cederberg G. (1998) *The Complete Book of Spinning and Baitcasting* Swan Hill
    Press
Miles T. (1996) *In Search of Big Chub* Crowood Press
Miles T. (2005) *My Way with Chub* Little Egret Press
Palmer B. (2005) *Dimples to Wrinkles and Beyond* Arima
Philips D. (1990) *Pike* Beekay
Pike Anglers Club (2000) *Pike Fishing Beyond 2000* PAC
Rickards B. (1992) *Success with Pike* David and Charles
Rickards B. and Bannister M. (2006) *The Great Modern Pike Anglers* Crowood Press
Rickards B. and Gay M. (1987) *The Pike Anglers Manual* A&C Black
Rogowski S. Ed. (2006) *Pike Fishing in the UK and Ireland* Crowood Press
Sidley J. (1990) *Eels* Beekay
Wakeford P. and Barrett M. Eds (2007) *PAC 30: A Celebration of 30 Years of the Pike Anglers
    Club of Great Britain* PAC
Walton I. (1653) *The Compleat Angler*
Willock C. Ed. (1992) *The New ABC of Fishing* Andre Deutsche
Winship B. Ed. (1990) *Pike Waters* Boydell
Younger S. (1996) *Fenland Zander* Tahjo

The Editor and Contributors

Steve Rogowski is an experienced pike angler who has caught pike in all of the countries of the British Isles, his personal best weighing just under 30 lb. He also enjoys fishing for eels, perch and zander, recently also having targeted catfish. He has written extensively about some of his experiences and is the editor of *Pike Fishing in the UK and Ireland*.

Mark Barrett has been interested in perch and perch fishing for many years, having caught many specimen-sized fish. He is also a keen pike and zander angler, currently being general secretary of the Pike Anglers Club. He has published widely about his angling experiences and is currently writing a book about fishing for zander.

Simon Clarke has fished for catfish for over twenty years, having caught many specimens in the process both in the British Isles and abroad. He is active in the Catfish Conservation Group and compiled their *Guide to UK Catfish Waters*, as well as establishing *Catfish-Pro* which provides a dedicated range of catfish tackle and accessories.

Neville Fickling, though perhaps primarily known as a pike angler and author, is also one of the best zander anglers and writers. He established the Zander Anglers Club in 1991 and has caught zander to over 15 lb, as well as pike to over 40 lb. He is joint editor of the Pike Anglers Club magazine *Pikelines*.

Steve Ormrod has had an interest in eels and eel fishing since the 1970s, having caught many specimens including to over the 5 lb mark. He is also a keen and enthusiastic pike angler who has had two stints of editing the Pike Anglers Club's magazine *Pikelines*. Most recently he has started targeting catfish. He has written many articles about his experiences.

Index